Something Fishy at Lake Iwannafisha

A Whodunnit Forensic Mystery

Available in print or eBook form.

Written by
Karen K. Schulz

Illustrated by
Taylor C. Schulz

Edited by
Patricia Gray

© 2018
THE CRITICAL THINKING CO.™
www.CriticalThinking.com
Phone: 800-458-4849 • Fax: 541-756-1758
1991 Sherman Ave., Suite 200 • North Bend • OR 97459
ISBN 978-1-60144-938-2

Printed in the United States of America by Gasch Printing, Odenton, MD (Aug. 2023)

About the Author

Karen Schulz is a master teacher with over 30 years of teaching experience. She was selected as Wildwood Middle School Teacher of the Year as well as the Rockwood School District Middle School Teacher of the Year. While working as a middle school gifted education teacher, she understood that students should be actively engaged in applying critical thinking skills in situations modeling real world experiences. This understanding led her to write *Something's Fishy at Lake Iwannafisha* to meet her students' needs.

Karen will be forever grateful to her students for letting her test out her material on them, her colleagues for field testing her curriculum, and her family for patiently listening to her while she rambled on about crime scene investigations. She resides in Ballwin, Missouri, with her husband Jim and their children Taylor and Matthew.

Dedication

This book is dedicated to the people I love the most—you'll find their names embedded within these pages. I would especially like to acknowledge:

- My father, Daniel Hartmann (1930–2013), who would have been pleased to see that our family business, Hartmann Farm Supply, est.1938, got a mention in this book.
- My mother, Patsy Hartmann, of whom I am so proud and who has unwavering faith in me and passionately believes that I can do anything.
- And of course, my husband Jim and our awesome children, Taylor and Matthew. Without a doubt, they are the source of my happiness.

Contents

HOW THIS CRIME INVESTIGATION WORKS

All student handouts are available in this book for copying or as PDFs at www.criticalthinking.com/iwannafisha

Something's fishy at Lake Iwannafisha. Human bones in the woods. A dead body in a burning shed. Counterfeit money in the fishing cabin. Throw in a couple of guns and a few bullets and you've got yourself a real mystery.

Students are actively engaged in this high interest simulation as they gather and analyze witness statements as well as forensic evidence to determine who is behind the deaths of two people, and who is making counterfeit money. Students will first learn about different types of forensic evidence such as fingerprints, ballistics, handwriting, and more. Using witness statements, police reports and forensic evidence lab reports, students must apply their critical thinking skills and forensic knowledge to solve this case.

Students, working in small teams, are initially given a police report along with two maps of the crime scene. It will be up to them to determine the path that they want to take as they work through the investigation. Will they ask to see a specific witness statement? If so, they will need to determine which information from the statement will be helpful to the investigation. Does the information lead them to another clue? Could the witness really be a suspect? Does this person have an alibi?

Perhaps they will ask to see a preliminary forensic report, such as a ballistics, fingerprint, or handwriting. These preliminary reports require students to use their forensic knowledge to analyze the information in the report, draw conclusions based on the content in the preliminary report, and record their findings in a final lab report. Their conclusions on the final reports will point them in the direction of the guilty parties.

The format of this simulation gives students the power to determine the course of action their investigation takes. As the investigation unfolds, and they determine what specific information they need, they will contact their sergeant (teacher) who will provide them with the requested materials. As with any investigation, students will need to make inferences and deal with the reality that not all loose ends are resolved. They will form conclusions based on witness statements, forensic reports, and other information revealed throughout the case.

If during the simulation the teams' investigations come to a standstill, you may need to prompt them. For example, if they don't know how to determine who the bones found at the shallow grave belong to, you might ask them what would happen in real life. Investigators would probably look to see if anyone has been reported missing. At that time, you could give the teams the Missing Persons report.

TEACHER INSTRUCTIONS

Overview of the Crimes at Lake Iwannafisha

The Hartmann fishing cabin, located on the outskirts of the city of Bass Lake, and overlooking Lake Iwannafisha, is being used by a counterfeit money ring. Tyler Terrington and his girlfriend, Patsy Bolen, rented the secluded cabin in 2016 to produce counterfeit money. At that time, Robbie Graber was walking the Catfish Trail leading behind the cabin. He stumbled onto their operation and was shot by Tyler Terrington. His body was buried in the woods behind the cabin. Jump forward to 2017. A blue Ford truck appears at the fishing cabin. The students will need to infer that the Ford truck found on the property belonged to Robbie Graber as evidenced by the DMV records containing the VIN as well as his fingerprint found on the steering wheel. Students might draw the conclusion that Tyler took the truck after killing Robbie in 2016 and drove the truck back to the cabin in 2017.

A year later, Tyler Terrington and Patsy Bolen are back for another round of making money. This time a neighbor, Andrew Hudson, discovered their operation and he was also killed by Tyler. Andrew's body was hidden in a shed on the property. Tyler kept Andrew's iPhone and it is later found in the cabin. Andrew's mother, worried about her son, continued to text and call him on the day he disappeared. When the counterfeiters saw a text from Andrew's mother saying she called the police and they were going to be looking for him, Tyler and Patsy panicked, started the shed on fire to cover the murder and sped away from the property in Patsy's car. Their quick get-a-away was witnessed by their neighbor, Taylor Daniels.

Patsy Bolen was also suspected of passing counterfeit money at a local gas station on the same day as the fire. Patsy denies starting the fire claiming she was in Bass Lake at the time. As indicated on the road sign on the location map, Bass Lake is 45 miles away from the fishing cabin. Students will need to deduce that Patsy, spotted at the Quik Trip at 8:45a.m., would have had enough time to make it back to the cabin by 9:45a.m., when the fire was reported. It is up to our team of detectives to prove that Tyler Terrington and Patsy Bolen are responsible for these crimes.

Profiles of the characters involved as witnesses, suspects, and missing persons are included for teacher reference. Also included are summaries of all of the reports that are available for students to reference. Note: These profiles and summaries are for teacher reference only, to give the teacher a general understanding of all of the characters involved in this simulation. The teacher will also have a better understanding of the information contained in each of the reports. DO NOT share these profiles and summaries with the students.

Witness Profiles

(For Teacher's Eyes Only)

Bass Lake Police Department Detective Jim Michaels	Bass Lake Police Department Officer Joseph Klipsch
• Wrote the report on the crime scene at the Hartmann fishing cabin which involved finding a dead body, human skeletal remains, and counterfeit money, to mention a few things.	• Wrote the report on the crime scene at the Quik Trip gas station which revealed counterfeit money was used to pay for gasoline.

Taylor Daniels	Matthew Hartmann	Michael Hartmann
• Lives at 111 Salmon Ln., Bass Lake, MO • On June 5, 2017 at 9:45a.m. called 911 after smelling and seeing smoke coming from the property behind her house • Saw a red car leaving the scene minutes afterwards • Remembers car from previous year • Heard pop/gun shots the day before, June 4	• Owns fishing cabin at 123 Trout Ln. as vacation home • Was there rehabbing the cabin May 10 – June 1, 2017 • Rents out cabin when not using it, but cabin was not currently rented • Gives record of who rented cabin, including their make of car and license plate number • Boat in front of cabin was not his • Truck found at shed was not his • Doesn't own a gun	• Lives in Millstadt Falls, MO • Rented the cabin Feb. 24 – March 2, 2016 • His daughters, Emily and Jessica, were with him • Drives a blue Ford truck, reported stolen in May 2017 • Between June 1 and 5, 2017, was at work and at home

Bella Hudson	Karen Kaye	Cheryl Young
• Mother of Andrew • Lives with Andrew at 15 Bluegill Lane, Bass Lake, MO • Went out of town to visit her sister on June 4, 2017 • Last saw her son fishing on June 4 as she left the house • Called/texted Andrew's cell phone repeatedly June 4 and June 5 but got no response from her son • Called BLPD on June 5 to file a missing person's report	• Manager at the Quik Trip in Bass Lake • Called 911 on June 5, 2017, at 8:50a.m. to report suspected counterfeit currency • Identified the car the suspected counterfeiter was driving as a red 4 door car with a dent in the back panel • Identified license plate of car as ABC321	• Lives in Baldwin, Illinois • Rented the fishing cabin with her husband Todd from Jan. 1 – Jan. 7, 2016 • Drives red Kia automobile • Between June 1–5, 2017, was working at family business • Not involved in crimes

Suspects Profiles

(For Teacher's Eyes Only)

Patsy Bolen	Tyler Terrington
• Lives in Millstadt Falls, MO • A red Honda Accord is registered to her with license plate number ABC321 • Denies being at the Hartmann fishing cabin between March 3 and 14, 2016 • Says her boyfriend may have used her car • Says she went to Bass Lake to shop at outlet malls on June 5, 2017, arriving there at 8:30a.m. and returning home by 5:00p.m. • Was seen at the Quik Trip in Bass Falls on June 5, 2017, at 8:45a.m. • Purchased gas with counterfeit money, the manager at gas station identified her car • Claims she was never at the fishing cabin on June 5, 2017, but Taylor Daniels witnessed Patsy's car leaving the fishing cabin about 9:45a.m. Note: Patsy claims it couldn't have been her car, as she was in Bass Lake, but Bass Lake is only 45 miles away so when Bolen left the QT, she could have made it back to the cabin in time. • Started the shed on fire • Was an accomplice (and girlfriend) to Tyler Terrington • Doesn't currently know the whereabouts of Tyler Terrington Forensic Reports • Handwriting matched writing on list found at crime scene • Fingerprints found on gas can found at shed • Fingerprints found on laser printer in the cabin	• Rented cabin March 3–March 14, 2016, and listed a red Honda Accord with license plate ABC321 as his car on the registration information • Was using the cabin as a secluded location to make counterfeit money • Killed Robbie Graber in 2016, when Robbie was walking the Catfish Trail and stumbled upon the counterfeit money making • Tyler buried Robbie's body in the woods behind the fishing cabin • Used cabin again in 2017 without renting it, broke in through a back window • Killed Andrew Hudson on June 4, 2017, when Andrew was fishing on Lake Iwannafisha, and found out about the counterfeiting • Put Andrew's body in shed on property Forensic Reports • Fingerprint found on gun in truck • Fingerprint found on gun under the front porch • Whereabouts currently unknown

Missing Persons Profiles

(For Teacher's Eyes Only)

Brendyn Caden	Andrew Hudson	Robbie Graber
• 21 years old • Caucasian, male • Last seen in the student union at Bass Lake University on March 10, 2016 • Roommate reported him missing when he didn't come home at night • Current whereabouts unknown • Red herring, not related to this crime	• 23 years old • African-American, male • Last seen fishing on Lake Iwannafisha on June 4, 2017 • His boat was later found in front of the fishing cabin • His cell phone was also found in the cabin • Reported missing by his mother, Bella Hudson, on June 5, 2017, when he did not answer her repeated calls and texts • Stumbled across the counterfeit money operation and was killed by Tyler Terrington • His body was found in the shed on the property of the fishing cabin (fits profile of Medical Examiner's report)	• 30 years old • Caucasian, male • Owns blue Ford truck, which is missing • Last seen hiking on Catfish Trail on March 4, 2016 • Girlfriend reported him missing when he didn't meet her for dinner that night • Stumbled across the counterfeit money operation and was killed by Tyler Terrington • His bones are the ones found in the woods behind the cabin (fits profile of anthropology report) • His truck was found next to the shed on the cabin property

Malik Monty	Alexa Ryan
• 24 years old • African-American, male • Last seen on June 1, 2017, leaving the Starbucks in Millstadt Falls. • Told the Starbucks barista that he was going to go hiking on the Catfish Trail • His car was never recovered • He was in town visiting his parents and they reported him missing when he never returned home • Current whereabouts unknown • Red herring (does fit profile of Medical Examiner's report, however, the time frame of life cycle of fly suggests body is not his, supported by Taylor Daniels' accounts of activity at Hartmann fishing cabin)	• 28 years old • Caucasian, female • Last seen driving out of the city of Bass Lake on January 14, 2016 • She was going to run errands, then go to mother's house • Never made it to her mother's house • Husband reported her missing • Current whereabouts unknown • Red herring, not related to this crime

Summaries of Police and Forensic Reports

(For Teacher's Eyes Only)

Crime Scene Report Case Number 033095 • Details information concerning crime scene at the Hartmann fishing cabin outside of Bass Lake	**Crime Scene Report Case Number 021394** • Details information concerning the passing of counterfeit money at the Quick Trip in Bass Lake.	**Anthropology** • Describes characteristics of the bones found in a shallow grave on the property of the cabin
Arson • Describes the scene of the fire, including a burn pattern, smoke and flame color, crazing found on windows, etc.	**Ballistics** • Details information about the bullets found in shed and in the grave • Details information about the guns found under porch and in truck • Includes a Firearms and Bullets Identification Catalog	**Counterfeit Money** • Describes features on money found at the cabin, as well as money recovered from the gas station
Department of Motor Vehicle • Provides the names of the owners of specific vehicles referenced in the cases • Provides information for each vehicle, including make, model, license plate number, VIN, etc.	**Document Examiner** • Provides a copy of the handwritten list left at the cabin • Includes a "12 Characteristics of Handwriting" guide • Includes handwriting samples from persons of interest	**Fingerprints** • Provides copies of the fingerprints recovered from the crime scene found on: ▪ steering wheel of truck ▪ gun under porch ▪ gun in truck ▪ gas can ▪ laser printer ▪ cell phone • Includes fingerprint samples from persons of interest
Medical Examiner • Autopsy results from examining the body found in the shed at the fishing cabin	**Missing Persons** • A profile of 5 people that have been reported missing in the Bass Lake area in the past year	

Timeline of Events

(For Teacher's Eyes Only)

2016

Jan. 1–Jan. 7	Cheryl Young and her husband Todd rented Hartmann's fishing cabin
January 14	Alexa Ryan last seen leaving her home in Bass Lake at 10:00 a.m.
January 15	Alexa Ryan reported missing
Feb. 22–March 2	Michael Hartmann rented the fishing cabin with daughters Emily and Jessica
March 3–March 14	Tyler Terrington rented the fishing cabin
March 4	Robbie Graber reported missing; last seen hiking the Catfish Trail at 9:00 a.m.
March 10	Brendyn Caden reported missing; last seen at Bass Lake University Student Union at 8:45 a.m.

2017

May 10–June 10	Hartmann fishing cabin closed for repairs
May 10–June 1	Matthew Hartmann at the cabin doing repairs/rehab
June 1–5	Cheryl and Todd Young were at home/work in Baldwin, Illinois
June 1–5	Michael Hartmann was at home/work in Millstadt Falls, Missouri
June 1–5	Matthew Hartmann was at home/work in Millstadt Falls, Missouri
June 1	Malik Monty reported missing; last seen leaving Starbucks in Bass Lake at 7:05 a.m.
June 4–5	Tyler Terrington and Patsy Bolen were at the Hartmann fishing cabin
June 4	Taylor Daniels heard popping noises—gun shots at approximately 12:30 p.m.
June 4	Bella Hudson last saw her son, Andrew, fishing at Lake Iwannafisha at 10:00 a.m.; called and texted him at 12:00 p.m., 2:00 p.m., 5:00 p.m., and 9:00 p.m., but got no response
June 5	Bella Hudson called/texted Andrew Hudson at 8:00 a.m., 9:00 a.m., and 9:30 a.m., and again got no response; called Bass Lake Police to report Andrew missing
June 5	Taylor Daniels called 911 at approximately 9:45 a.m. to report seeing smoke at the fishing cabin
June 5	Patsy Bolen was seen at Quik Trip in Bass Lake at approximately 8:45 a.m.; accused of paying for gas with counterfeit money; her car was reportedly seen leaving the Hartmann fishing cabin approximately 1 hour later.
June 5	Bass Lake PD responded to a call to the Hartmann fishing cabin; crime scene findings are detailed in Case Number 033095 report.

Step-By-Step Instructions

1. In order for students to solve these cases, they will need background information on the following forensic topics: anthropology, arson, ballistics, counterfeit money, death investigation, document and handwriting analysis, and fingerprints. Handouts [see Forensic Evidence Lessons (page 1)] are provided covering each topic. Students should be given this information prior to introducing the simulation, so make copies and give them to the students, or make the information available to them through a source such as Google Classroom.

2. A student can work alone or in groups of 3 or 4 students. For each group, you will need the following handouts:

    - Case File Introduction (Page 27)
    - Crime Scene Location Map (Page 28)
    - Crime Scene Evidence Map (Page 29)
    - Crime Scene Report Case 033095 (Pages 30-31)
    - Investigation Notes for Case File 033095 (Pages 32-35)
    - Witness Interview Notes—1 copy Categories (Page 36) plus 7 copies of the Witness Interview Notes blank form (Page 37)
    - Person of Interest Profiles—1 copy Categories (Page 38) plus 3 copies
    - Person of Interest Profile blank form (Page 39)
    - Missing Persons Report (Pages 40-41)
    - Crime Scene Report Case 021394 (Page 42)
    - Investigation Notes for Case File 021394 (Pages 43-44)
    - Timeline of Events 2016/2017 (Pages 45-46)
    - Case Closed: Final Report Cases 021394 and 033095 (Pages 47-50)
    - Witness Statements (Pages 53-67)
    - Forensic Lab Preliminary and Final Reports (Pages 68-112)

    All student handouts are available in this book for copying or as PDFs at www.criticalthinking.com/iwannafisha

3. Give each group a two-pocket folder to hold their reports and other paperwork. The folders should initially just contain the following handouts:

    - Cases File Introduction (Page 27)
    - Crime Scene Report Case 033095 (Pages 30-31)
    - Investigation Notes for Case file 033095 (Pages 32-35)
    - Crime Scene Maps (Pages 28-29)

4. For organizational purposes, put the remaining handouts in a folder designated specifically for each group. As the group asks for additional pieces of evidence, pull it out of their folder. That should make it easier to keep track of how each group is working through the case.

Keep track of the handouts you've given each group by marking them on the Checklist for Handouts (Page xix).

5. Hand each group their prepared folder and explain to them that they will be investigating a case. The only information they have to start with is located in the folder. Together, read the Case File Introduction handout. They will need to carefully read the Crime Scene Report Case 033095 and look at both maps. They should then complete the Investigation Notes handout (Pages 32-35) to help them process the information and develop a plan of action.

6. After students have completed the Investigation Notes handouts and have a plan of action, they should come to you, their sergeant (teacher), and request information. They might say that they want to interview Matthew Hartmann, the owner of the cabin, or perhaps they will want to talk to the neighbor, Taylor Daniels, who called 911. Whomever they request, just give them one witness statement at a time. Be sure to give them the Witness Interview Notes blank form (Page 37) each time you give them a witness statement so they can record notes as they go. Note: Should they ask for a witness statement and you do not have one, you can simply say, "We have not been able to locate this person for an interview, or just simply say "We do not have his testimony on file." For example, groups may ask to interview Tyler Terrington, but a witness statement doesn't exist for him, because the police have not been able to track him down, which is an important part of the storyline.

7. Groups might also decide to see if any fingerprints were left behind and request a fingerprint report. If they ask for the fingerprint report, give them the Preliminary Report to begin with. Don't give them the Fingerprint reports for the individual suspects until they specifically identify a person as a suspect. Many students simply will say, "Can we see any fingerprints you have on file?" Respond by telling them that investigators don't ask to see the fingerprints of every living person. Some people don't even have their fingerprints on file. Students should ask for the prints of a specific individual who they believe might be involved in the case. This should be the format you follow no matter what type of evidence/report they ask for. You have the ability to control the release of information, so you will have to decide when you want to release specific reports. It may vary with each group.

8. Keep in mind the preliminary forensic reports reflect information about what was found at the crime scene. Each forensic report has a final report that asks students to draw conclusions based on their forensic knowledge. It is on this final report that they will apply the information and demonstrate mastery from the forensic lessons you previously taught them. Note: Should they ask for evidence that you do not have (for example, fingerprints for Taylor Daniels) simply say, "We do not have a record of her fingerprints on file." As the group proceeds through their investigation they will realize that Taylor Daniels is not a suspect, and therefore, there is no need to see her fingerprints. Do not announce that she is not a suspect, but rather have the students draw their own conclusions.

9. Students should continue to work through the evidence and witness' statements until they

have received all information. At some point in time, early in the investigation, you should give them the Crime Scene Report Case 021394 (Page 42) and the Investigation Notes for Case File 021394 (Pages 43-44), which details the passing of counterfeit money at the Quik Trip gas station. Students will not be directed to this information anywhere in their investigation, so you will have to announce that a crime has been committed that might be related to the crime they are investigating. Hand them the report and let them determine any possible links.

10. When groups start to generate a list of people they suspect, provide them with the Person of Interest Profile blank forms (Page 39). In addition, distribute the Timeline of Events 2016/2017 form (Pages 45-46). Since the crimes committed span the course of two years, students may find it helpful to document the time frame of the various events. Completing these forms will help the students organize and justify their thoughts.

11. When students believe they are ready to charge someone with the crime(s), give them the Case Closed: Final Report Case Numbers 021394 and 033095 (Pages 47-50). They will use this form to summarize the case. You may ask them to turn this in for a final grade.

12. As in a real investigation, there may be loose ends. Some of the evidence found or the people interviewed or listed as missing may have nothing to do with this case. This may be bothersome to some students, but realistically, this happens in actual investigations. Students may also feel like they need additional information that is not provided. Again, this is often a reality in many investigations.

13. At the end of the simulation, it is important to do a debriefing with the students. See the Case Debriefing handout (Page 51) for suggested discussion topics.

Helpful Tips

1. Throughout this simulation, students will receive a lot of handouts. Provide groups with paper clips, sticky notes, and any other materials that will help them organize their handouts.

2. You may suggest to students that they use highlighters and actively annotate as they are reading each report. Annotating is a good skill to practice, and it will help them pull out the most important pieces of information.

3. Running the final reports on a different color of paper might be helpful, particularly if you are going to be grading their final reports. This makes it easy for the kids to understand what they have to turn in at the end of the simulation. For example, anything copied on color paper should be turned in.

Checklist for Handouts Group ____________________

Teacher copy—Check off each handout as you distribute them to the designated group. All student handouts are available in this book for copying or as PDFs at www.criticalthinking.com/iwannafisha

Crime Scene Reports and General Forms

_____ Case File Introduction
_____ Crime Scene Maps (location/evidence)
_____ Crime Scene Report Case 033095
_____ Crime Scene Report Case 021394
_____ Investigation Notes for Case File 033095
_____ Timeline of Events 2016/2017
_____ Missing Persons Reports
_____ Investigation Notes for Case File 021394
_____ Case Closed: Final Report Cases 021394 and 033095

Witness Statements

_____ Witness Interview Notes Categories
_____ Patsy Bolen
_____ Taylor Daniels
_____ Matthew Hartmann
_____ Michael Hartmann
_____ Bella Hudson
_____ Karen Kaye
_____ Cheryl Young

Person of Interest Profiles

_____ Categories
_____ Blank Form

Lab Reports—Anthropology Case 033095

_____ Preliminary Report
_____ Final Report

Lab Reports—Arson Case 033095

_____ Preliminary Report
_____ Final Report

Lab Reports—Case 033095

_____ Ballistics Preliminary Report (part 1)
_____ Ballistics Final Report (part 1)
_____ Firearms Identification Catalog and Bullets Identification Catalog (part 1)
_____ Firearms Reports #1 and #2 (part 2)
_____ Striations Reports #1, #2, and #3 (part 2)

Lab Reports—Counterfeit Currency

_____ Preliminary Report Case 021394
_____ Final Report Case 021394
_____ Preliminary Report Case 033095
_____ Final Report Case 033095

Department of Motor Vehicles Registrations

_____ Patsy Bolen
_____ Robbie Graber
_____ Michael Hartmann
_____ Cheryl Young

Lab Reports—Document and Handwriting Case 033095

_____ Preliminary Report
_____ Final Report
_____ 12 Handwriting Characteristics
_____ Patsy Bolen Handwriting Sample
_____ Matthew Hartmann Handwriting Sample
_____ Michael Hartmann Handwriting Sample
_____ Cheryl Young Handwriting Sample

Lab Reports—Fingerprints Case 033095

_____ Preliminary Report
_____ Final Report
_____ Patsy Bolen Fingerprint Card
_____ Robbie Graber Fingerprint Card
_____ Matthew Hartmann Fingerprint Card
_____ Michael Hartmann Fingerprint Card
_____ Andrew Hudson Fingerprint Card
_____ Monte Malik Fingerprint Card
_____ Tyler Terrington Fingerprint Card
_____ Cheryl Young Fingerprint Card

Lab Reports—Medical Examiner Case 033095

_____ Preliminary Report
_____ Final Report

FORENSIC EVIDENCE LESSONS

Anthropology

Forensic anthropology is the study of skeletal remains (bones) in order to determine gender, age, race, marks of trauma, etc. in relation to a crime.

During the process of their examination, forensic anthropologists ask the following questions:

1. Is it bone? Is it human?
2. What bones are present?
3. How many people are represented?
4. Are the remains modern or ancient?
5. What happened? When did it happen?
6. Who is the individual/profile (sex, age, race, height)?

Determining Age

An adult human has 206 bones. A newborn baby has 305 bones. In young humans, bones vary in number with age as the bones develop, grow, and fuse together. Looking at the number of bones can be used to approximate age.

A variety of bones may be used to help estimate the approximate age of the person to whom the bones belong.

Hand Bones	Baby Hand	Adult Hand
Notice the separation of the bones in the image of the hand of a baby. As we get older, the bones will fuse together to form a single bone as shown in the image of the adult hand.	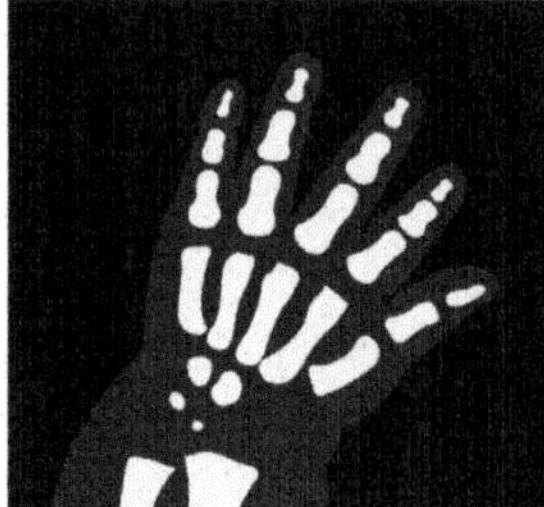	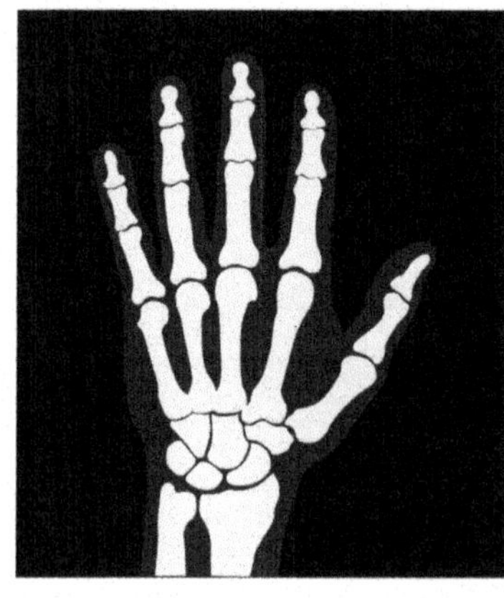

Knee Bones

Notice the lines between the longer shafts (the diaphysis) of the bone and the tips (the epiphysis).

During childhood and the teenage years, the diaphysis and epiphysis will fuse together.

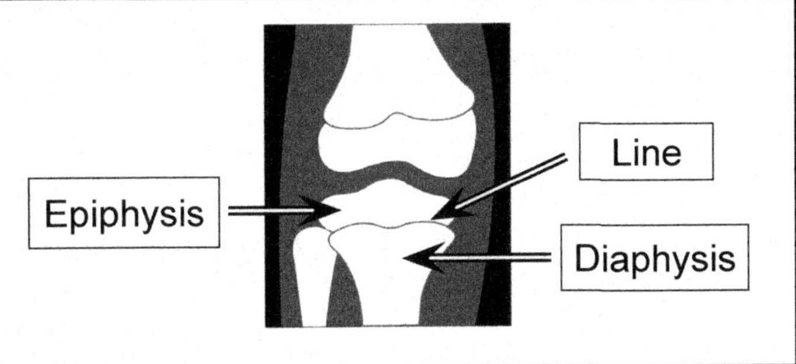

Important age indicators are also the sutures located on the skull.

The bones of the skull come together along special serrated and interlocking joints known as sutures. The sutures allow for growth of the skull.

During adulthood, bone "remodeling" may gradually erase these lines at various rates, which then gives general information about a person's age.

Skull

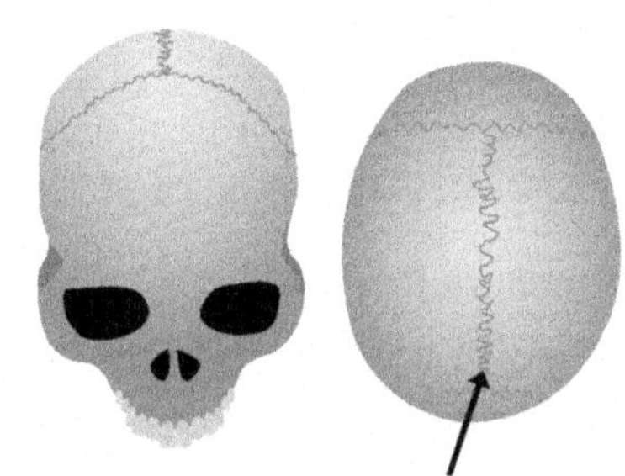

Sagittal suture

The sagittal suture is located along the top of the skull, dividing it from right to left.

It runs from the top of the skull to the middle of the back of the skull.

If this suture is completely closed, then a male would be at least 26 years of age or older. A female would be 29 years of age or older.

Determining Gender

Determining gender (sex) is crucial when analyzing unidentified human remains. In general, men's bones are larger. There are several other bones used for identifying gender.

Pelvic Bones

The pelvic bones have the most obvious differences between men and women.

Males have a narrow long sacrum. Females have a broader pubic arch and a wider pelvic outlet.

Female **Male**

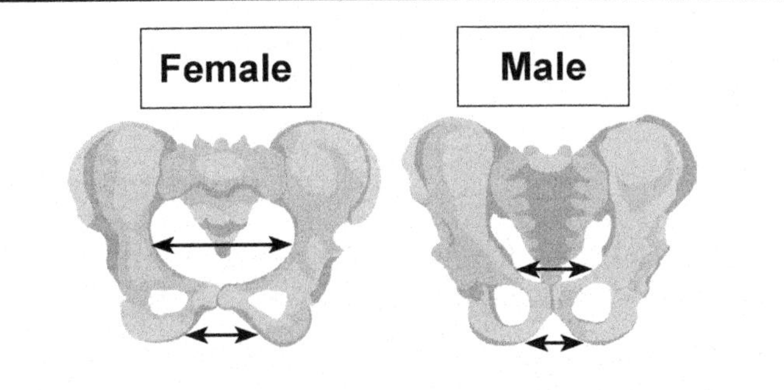

Determining Gender: Primary Differences in Skulls Between Males and Females

Feature	Male	Female
Eye Openings	Tend to be more square, small	Tend to be more round, large
Brow Ridges	Prominent and heavy	Smooth, flat
Chin	Tend to be U-shaped	Tend to be V-shaped
Forehead	Sloping, less round	Vertical, fuller

Determining Race

To determine race, anthropologists examine the shape of the skull, taking measurements of the skull and face. They compare these results with data from populations worldwide and evaluate that individual's relationship to a world group. This allows anthropologists to draw conclusions about a person's race.

Determining Race: Primary Differences in Skulls

Feature	Caucasoid	Negroid	Mongoloid
Skull Shape	Small, rounded	Long, large	Rounded, large
Cranial Length	Long	Long	Short
Cranial Breadth	Narrow	Narrow	Broad
Cranial Height	Medium to high	Low	Medium to high
Eye Orbits	Sloping	Rectangular	Rounded
Nasal Aperture	Narrow	Inverted heart	Round
Chin	Prominent	Vertical	Vertical

Using Length of Bones to Determine Height

There is a close relationship between the length of a person's arm and leg to his height. When examining an unidentified arm or leg bone, anthropologists can measure the arm and/or leg bones and put the measurements into a mathematical formula to determine the approximate height of the person to whom the bone belongs.

Determining Height

Using Length of Bones to Determine Height

The most commonly used bones in estimating height are the femur and the humerus, although the tibia and fibula may also be used. Estimating how tall someone is can help identify an unknown individual when certain bones are found.

The formulas listed below are used. Note there are different formulas used for males and females.

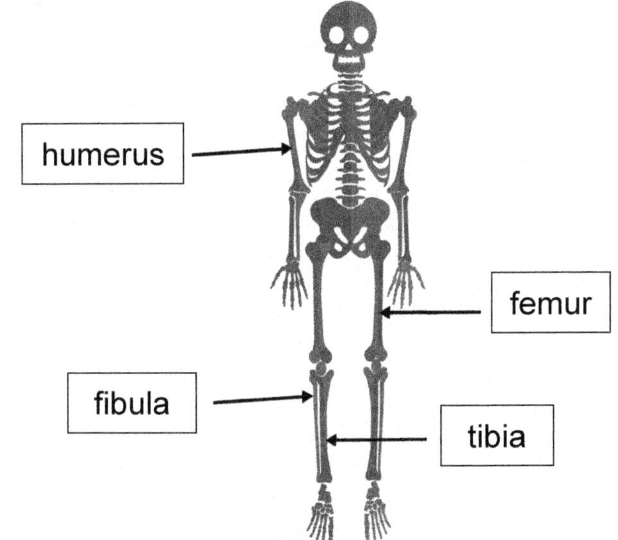

Formulas for Estimating Height for Males (in centimeters)	Formulas for Estimating Height for Females (in centimeters)
Height = **femur** length x 2.27 + 67.99	Height = **femur** length x 2.38 + 57.13
Height = **tibia** length x 2.37 + 80.97	Height = **tibia** length x 2.68 + 65.63
Height = **fibula** length x 2.44 + 78.36	Height = **fibula** length x 2.71 + 65.26
Height = **humerus** length x 2.99 + 72.42	Height = **humerus** length x 3.22 + 61.32

Steps to Determine Height of Person With Femur Measuring 42 cm	Male	Female
1. Identify the type of bone and plug it into the correct formula. (Calculate both male and female if the gender is unknown.)	H = **42** x 2.27 + 67.99	H = **42** x 2.38 + 57.13
2. Solve the equation to calculate the height in centimeters.	H = 163.33 cm	H= 157.09 cm
3. Convert centimeters to inches (1 in. = 2.54cm)	163.33/2.54 = 64.3 inches (round to the nearest whole number) 64 inches	157.09/2.54 = 61.84 62 inches
4. Convert inches to feet and inches	64/12 = 5 feet 4 inches	62/12 = 5 feet 2 inches
Conclusion: A femur measuring 42 cm could belong to a male with an approximate height of 5 feet 4 inches or a female who is about 5 feet 2 inches tall.		

Arson

Arson

An intentionally set fire to a house, building, or other property.

Point of Origin

The location where the fire started.

Accelerants

Anything that makes the fire burn faster and hotter, such as gasoline, paint thinner, alcohol, and other chemicals.

Crazing (cracks)

Small cracks on glass indicate a fast, hot fire, which means an accelerant was used to start a fire.

Large cracks on glass indicate a slow fire, which means an accelerant was not used.

Fire Patterns

Unique patterns made by the fire while it burns. Fire patterns are formed when the products of combustion come into contact with a vertical or horizontal surface such as a wall, floor, ceiling, or home furnishing. Patterns can show the origin and path of a fire.

Flames are conical in shape and so when a fire hits a wall, it will flame up in a V-pattern, which points to the area of fire origin. A wide U-shape or random shape could indicate that there was a "pool of origin" instead of a "point." For example, it may have been started by someone spreading gasoline around a large area.

Temperatures Associated With a Fire

1,200°F: Aluminum melts

1,550°F: A normal house fire burns

1,981°F: Copper melts

2,781°F: Steel melts

In a normal house fire, you would expect anything aluminum to melt. If copper and steel melt, an accelerant was used.

Temperatures Associated With Flame Color

900 °F: Faint red

1,050 °F: Blood red

1,550 °F: Bright red (normal house fire)

1,725 °F: Orange

1,825 °F: Lemon

2,200 °F: White

2,250 °F: Blue white

Smoke Color Associated With Combustibles

White: Phosphorous

Yellow: Sulfur, sulfuric acid, gunpowder

Gray to brown: Wood, paper, cloth

Brown: Cooking oil

Brownish black: Lacquer thinner

Black: Acetone, kerosene, gasoline, tar, coal

Rate at Which Wood Burns

Wood burns at the rate of approximately 1 inch in 45 minutes. Investigators can use this information to determine how long a fire has been burning.

Arson Motives

There are multiple reasons why someone would intentionally start a fire.

Civil disorder: When people are protesting certain conditions, their actions sometimes result in burning down a church, a government building, or other such establishments.

Crime concealment: Using a fire to hide a theft or other crime.

Insurance fraud: People may start a fire for financial gain or to offset the losses from a failing business.

Juvenile: Kids under the age of 16 who start a fire for "fun."

Pyromania: A person who enjoys setting fires and gets a thrill out of seeing things burn.

Spite or revenge: When someone is very angry, he or she may burn down someone's house or business to get revenge.

Vanity: A person starts a fire because he or she wants to be the hero, save people, or get public recognition.

Ballistics

Ballistics

The study of a projectile in motion as it relates to a criminal investigation.

The area of forensic science in which experts determine if a bullet, cartridge case, or other ammunition component was fired by a particular firearm.

Experts

- Compare bullets and/or cartridge cases to firearms
- Sort and examine evidence for class characteristics, including looking for rifling pattern
- Test fire firearms and compare evidence to tests
- Examine and analyze:
    - Firearms/guns
    - Shell casings/bullets
    - Gunshot residue
    - Trajectories to determine the distance and the angle from which a bullet was fired

Firing a Gun: Rifling and Striations

When a bullet is fired through a rifled barrel, the raised and lowered spirals of the rifling etch fine grooves called striations into the bullet. These marks are unique to each individual gun. Just like fingerprints, no two firearms will produce the same marks or striations, even those of the same make and model.

Experts are able use these striations to trace a bullet back to the gun that fired it.

Rifling

Consists of spiral grooves in the barrel of a gun or firearm. The spiral grooves leave "lands" or high parts, intact between them.

These grooves cause the bullet to spin, which improves the aerodynamic stability and accuracy of the fired bullet.

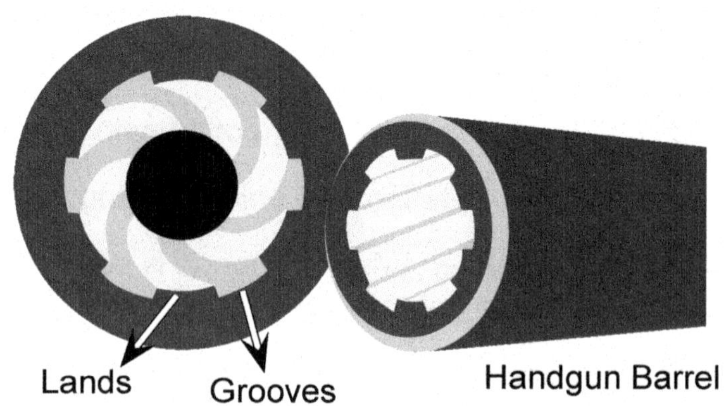

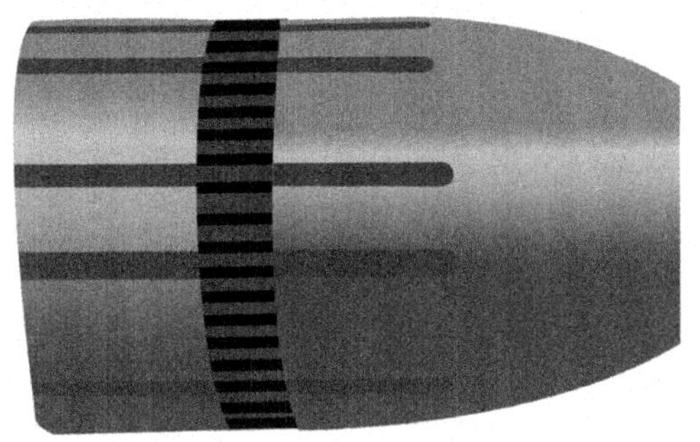

Striations

The rifling of each weapon leaves its unique pattern of marks or scratches (striations) on the bullet.

Striations run parallel to the length of the bullet.

Identification Using Striations

When bullets are gathered from a crime scene, they are sent to the ballistic lab for examination. Experts first determine the caliber (width) of the bullet to determine what type of gun it may have been fired from.

If investigators believe they have the gun that was involved in the crime, they will first see if the caliber of the bullet they gathered could have been fired from the questioned gun.

Next, they perform a test to determine if the pattern of striations found on the bullet match the pattern of rifling contained in the barrel of the questioned firearm.

Testing the Gun to Compare Striations

In order to get a sample bullet for comparison, the gun in question will be fired in a special tank of water.

The barrel of the gun is inserted in the open tube at the end of the tank and fired.

As the bullet passes through the water, it slows down and then the bullet is recovered from the bottom of the tank.

After the bullet is removed, the striations of this bullet are compared to the striations on the bullet recovered from the crime scene.

Striation Comparison

A comparison microscope is used to compare the striations of the two bullets side-by-side.

If the striations match, then experts can conclude that this gun fired the bullet that was at the crime scene.

Bullet Found at Crime Scene	Bullet Tested at Lab

Side-By-Side Comparison

Images of the striations are placed side-by-side in a computer program to determine whether or not they are a match.

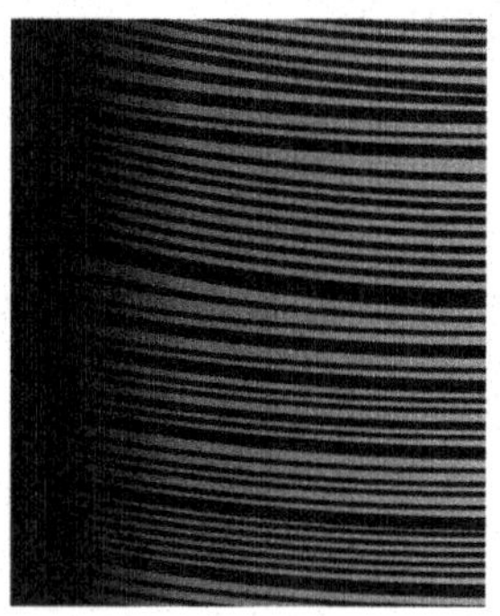

Bullet Found at Crime Scene

Bullet Tested at Lab

Counterfeit Money

The **Bureau of Engraving and Printing (BEP)** is one of the largest money printing operations in the world, with offices in Washington, DC, and Fort Worth, Texas.

Money is also known as "notes," "bills," or "currency."

The **BEP** produces 38 million notes a day with a face value of about $541 million.

95% of the notes printed each year are used to replace notes already in circulation. The old notes are destroyed.

The average note costs 10 cents to make.

The Federal Reserve System is often simply referred to as "the Fed". They are the central bank of the United States.

It was created by Congress to provide the nation with a safer, more flexible, and more stable monetary and financial system.

The **Secret Service** is the branch of government that investigates the production and use of counterfeit money.

Note: The role of the Secret Service was later expanded to include protecting government officials.

Counterfeit money is imitation or fake money, made without the approval of the government. It is illegal for individuals to produce and spend.

It is used with the intention to deceive someone. The most commonly counterfeited bill is the $20 bill.

United States Currency: Security Features

Money is created with special security features that are difficult and often impossible to duplicate.

When examining a note, investigators look at many security features to determine the authenticity of the currency.

- Type of paper
- Watermark
- Color shifting ink
- Security thread
- Embedded red/blue fibers
- Micro-printing

Type of Paper

Notes are made out of 25% linen and 75% cotton. When touching a questionable note, one should be able to tell a real one from a counterfeit note, based on the way the note feels.

The paper also contains randomly disbursed red and blue security fibers embedded throughout the bill.

Type of Ink

Inks appearing on U.S. currency are specially formulated and blended by the BEP.

All bills use green ink on the backs.

Faces or fronts of the bill use black ink, color-shifting ink, and metallic ink.

Color Shifting Ink

The $10, $20, $50, and $100 bills include color shifting ink. When the note is tilted 45 degrees, the ink shifts from a copper to a green color.

The $1 and $5 bills do not have color shifting ink, as they are not commonly counterfeited.

Watermark

A watermark is a faint design made in a bill when the bill is manufactured. It is visible from either side of the note when held up to a light source. The watermark matches the portrait on the bill.

The notes that have a watermark are the $5, $10, $20, $50, and $100 bills.

Security Thread

All notes except the $1 bill have a clear thread embedded vertically in the paper. The thread is inscribed with the denomination of the note and is visible only when held to a UV light. Each denomination has a unique thread position and glows a different color:

$5—blue $10—orange $20—green

$50—yellow $100—pink

3D Security Ribbon

The $100 note features a blue ribbon woven into the paper.

When you tilt the note back and forth, the "bells" and the "100s" move side to side.

If you tilt the note side to side, they move up and down.

Micro-Printing

Teeny-tiny words or numbers are written on the bills which makes them hard to clearly photocopy. The words/letters become blurry when copied. Go to https://www.uscurrency.gov to see examples of micro-printing on the various denominations.

Making Counterfeit Money

Most counterfeiters don't produce an exact copy of a bill, but rather they want to make a bill that looks close enough to the real thing so that the money can be passed without detection.

Counterfeit money is most often printed on color copiers and printers, which means the money is copied on regular, wood-based printer paper. This paper contains starch.

Keep in mind that real money is printed on a combination of linen and cotton—very different from printer paper. Real money does not contain any starch. For this reason, it is easy to detect a counterfeit bill by using a counterfeit detection pen.

Some counterfeiters will bleach real $1 bills and then print a new denomination on top of the real paper.

Counterfeit Detection Pen

Using the counterfeit detection pen is extremely simple. The ink in the pen contains an iodine solution that reacts with the starch in wood-based paper to create a black stain.

Whenever the pen is brushed across counterfeit currency, a black mark will remain.

This signals that the paper is wood-based and not cotton/fiber so therefore the bill is a fake.

When the pen is applied to the fiber-based paper used in real money, the mark is yellowish or sometimes even colorless.

Security Features—A Closer Look

United States paper bills are redesigned as a way to protect the legitimacy of money. Technology is always advancing, which gives counterfeiters new ways to make fake money. Most bills have the following security features: (1) watermark, (2) color shifting ink, (3) security thread, (4) 3D security ribbon, and (5) serial numbers.

To learn more about the safety features and to see these features animated on the various denominations, check out the following website:

https://www.uscurrency.gov

Death Investigation

Forensic Entomology

Death Scene Investigation

A forensic entomologist helps with the when and the where.

A medical examiner or pathologist helps with the who and how, and determines if it is natural, accidental, or criminal.

Questions Asked During a Death Scene Investigation

Who is the deceased?

How did the death occur?

When and where did the death occur?

Is the death natural, accidental, or criminal?

Insects and Their Relation to a Criminal Investigation

A forensic entomologist is a scientist who studies insects and their relation to a criminal investigation.

Insects are used to estimate the time of death by looking at the life cycle of certain insects as well as environmental conditions.

The most common and useful insect to study in death investigations is the common fly, although other bugs, such as the beetle, may also be examined.

Postmortem Interval (PMI)

PMI is the length of time between the death and the discovery of the corpse.

Clues left from bugs help determine the PMI of bodies found at crime scenes.

Determining Time of Death

Insects arrive in a predictable order and are usually the first to discover a corpse.

In outdoor cases, flies arrive and lay eggs on the body within minutes of death.

Knowing the life cycle of flies can help establish a time frame for death.

Life Cycle of Insects

Entomologists use this life cycle to calculate when a victim died based on the stage of the flies when the body is discovered.

Life Cycle of Insects

Looking at the oldest stage of the insect and the temperature of the region, one can estimate the day or range of days in which the first insects laid eggs and provide an estimated time of death.

This method applies until the first adults emerge. After this, it is impossible to determine which generation is present.

The time since death must be estimated from insect succession.

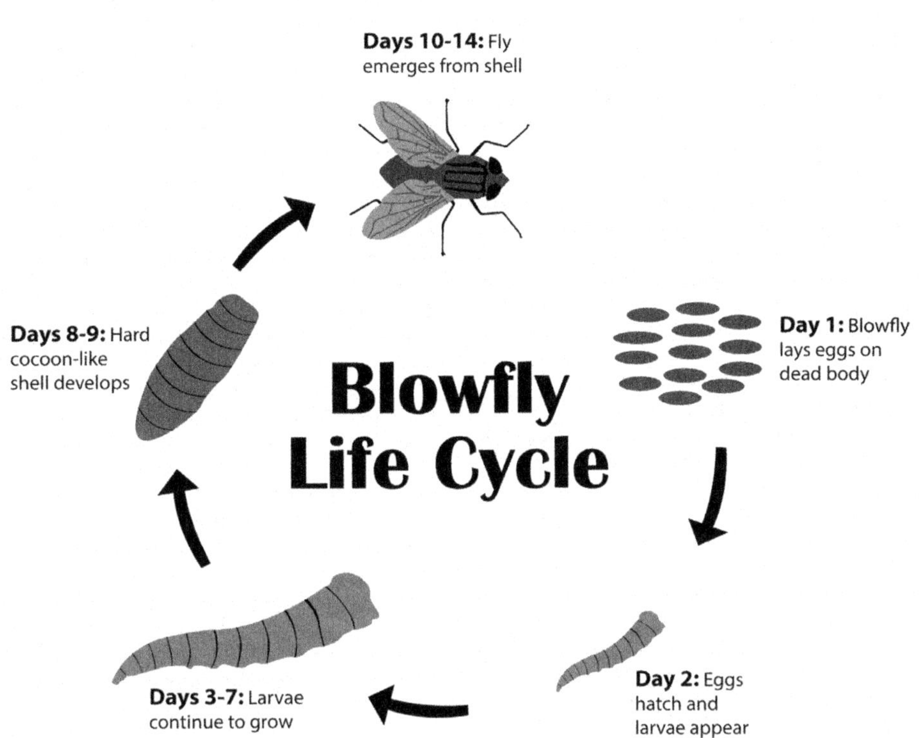

Determining Place of Death

Species of insects/flies may only live in certain areas, so this can point to events that occurred after death. For example, you would expect a common blowfly to be present on a body found in Missouri. An absence of this fly could raise a red flag for investigators.

The presence of insects on the body that are not found in the area suggests the body was moved. Those insects may indicate the type of area where the murder took place. For example, if a species that is normally found only in the countryside is found at a scene in the city, it suggests the body has been moved at some point after death.

Determining Time of Death Isn't Easy

Environmental temperatures can impact the decomposition and overall condition of the body.

Cold weather can slow down the decomposition process, and insects may not be present in freezing weather.

Hot weather can also make a body decay faster and increase insect activity.

Forensic Autopsy

Forensic Autopsy

A forensic autopsy is a medical procedure performed on a body after death to evaluate the cause of death.

If a death is determined to be unexpected, unusual, or unnatural, an autopsy will be performed by a doctor called a pathologist or medical examiner.

Categories of Death

Natural: Old age, heart failure, cancer

Accident: Car crash, bad fall

Suicide: Someone takes their own life

Undetermined: Can't establish a cause

Homicide: Murder

Medical Examiner (ME)

An ME is both a doctor and a crime scientist who knows how to examine and interpret injuries as evidence. He can explain what the injuries prove or don't prove about the person's death. The ME is called to investigate in situations such as these:

- Cases of violence
- An unidentified or unclaimed body
- A death involving alcohol, drugs, or other toxins
- A sudden death that can't be explained

Determining Time of Death

This can be tricky because of the many factors and conditions that affect the body at the time of death such as:

- Is the body buried, or in the open? In water or on land?
- Is the weather hot or cold? Rainy or dry?

Corpses do change over time according to basic laws of science, which include livor mortis and rigor mortis.

Livor Mortis

- Means "death color," it is the discoloration of skin due to the pooling of blood after death
- As a body begins to decompose, blood seeps down and settles in lower parts of the body
- The blood cells turn a purplish-blue color

Rigor Mortis

Rigor Mortis is called "death stiffness" because skeletal muscles are locked into a flexed position and are unable to relax after death. This usually starts within two hours of death. At 12 hours, the body is at most rigid state. Stiffness usually disappears after 38 hours, but can remain for up to 48 hours.

Factors impacting rigor mortis:

Temperature: Colder temps slow down the rigor process, while warm temps increase the process.

Clothing: A clothed body makes rigor occur faster, while being unclothed slows the rigor.

Body weight: Obesity slows rigor, while being thin increases the rate of rigor.

Sun: Exposure accelerates the rate of rigor.

Autopsy Process

1. An external exam is completed first.
2. Photos and x-rays may be taken. This will confirm injuries; locate bruises, bullets, or other objects; and find any abnormalities.
3. Gunshot entrance and exit wounds are examined to determine position of shooter.
4. Trace evidence is collected.
5. Body is weighed and measured.
6. Location and description of identifying marks are taken (such as tattoos, birthmarks, scars, etc.).
7. The organs are examined for signs of trauma or disease.
8. Samples of blood and body fluids may be removed and preserved to test for drugs, infection, or other chemicals.
9. The medical examiner completes and signs the cause of death on the death certificate.

Examination of Organs During an Autopsy

Lungs: Fire Victim

If smoke is found in the lungs, it means the person was alive and breathing while in the fire.

If smoke is not found in the lungs, it means the person did not breathe in the smoke and must have been dead before the fire started.

Lungs: Drowning Victim

If water is found in the lungs, it means the person was alive and breathing while in the water and must have drowned.

If water is not found in the lungs, it means the person did not inhale any water and must have been dead before being placed in the water.

Stomach Content

If there is undigested food in the stomach then death occurred 0-2 hours after the last meal.

If the stomach is empty, but food is found in small intestine, then death occurred at least 4-6 hours after the last meal.

If the small intestine is empty, but there is food/waste in the large intestine, then death occurred 12 or more hours after the last meal.

It takes 24 hours for all undigested food from a meal to leave the body as waste.

Cause of Death

Determining the cause of death and estimating the time of death are very beneficial in any criminal investigation.

They offer up valuable clues as to the last moments or hours of an individual's life before he/she died.

Document and Handwriting Analysis

Document/Handwriting Examiner

This is an expert who examines handwriting and documents, including paper and ink, to determine authenticity.

Answers questions such as:

- Is the document real or forged?
- Who wrote it?

Document/Handwriting Cases

Most cases involve an unknown (questioned) writing sample being compared with a sample from a known writer.

The goal is to determine whether the same person wrote both samples.

Questioned Document

This is any signature, handwriting, or other mark whose source or authenticity is in dispute or doubtful.

This could be any document about which some issue has been raised or that is the subject of an investigation.

Forgery

This is a document made with the intent to deceive.

Example documents include: wills, checks, baseball cards (including autographed), and stamps.

The most common forgery is a signature.

Types of Forgery		
Blind Forgery	**Simulated Forgery**	**Traced Forgery**
Most common and easiest to detect. The forger uses his/her own handwriting. He/she doesn't even know what the actual signature looks like.	Very difficult to link to a suspect. The forger practices writing the signature so much that he or she can carefully draw/write it. Must have access to the real signature.	Line quality is inconsistent. The forger traces a real signature using a light box or other device. Must have access to the real signature.

Class Characteristics

Many writing habits carry over until adulthood and are called class characteristics. This uniqueness gives our handwriting individual characteristics that makes it different from others. The way we write becomes so subconscious that it is actually quite difficult for us to disguise. An expert looks for class characteristic differences when examining handwriting samples. However, as we get older, we develop our own unique distinctions in our writing.

To determine whether a signature or writing is real, an examiner will look for the 12 characteristics for comparing handwriting below.

1. Line Quality Are the lines: • smooth? • shaky? • juvenile? • deliberate?	**2. Spacing of Words and Letters** Is the spacing of words and letters on the page consistent between the known and questioned document?	**3. Ratio of Relative Height, Width, and Size of Letters** Are the height, width, and size of the letters consistent between the known and questioned document?
4. Pen Lifts and Separations Check how the writer stops to form new letters and begins words	**5. Connecting Strokes** Compare how capital letters are connected to lowercase letters and how strokes connect between letters and between words	**6. Beginning and Ending Strokes** Compare how the writer begins and ends a word, number, or letter. Are the strokes straight, curled, long, or short?
7. Unusual Letter Formation Look for unusual letter formation: • Letters written backwards • Letters with a tail • Unusual capitals	**8. Shading or Pen Pressure** Individuals use different amounts of pressure with a pen or pencil, making the lines darker or wider.	**9. Slant** Does the writing slant to the right or left, or is it straight up or down?
10. Baseline Habits Does the writing tend to follow a straight line, move downward, or move upward? Is it above or below the line?	**11. Flourishes or Embellishments** Are there any fancy letters, curls, loops, circles, etc.	**12. Placement of Diacritics** Check the crossing of t's and dotting of the i's, j's ,etc. For example, is the line on the "t" long in proportion to the stem? Is it located to the left or right? Slanted?

Fingerprints

Fingerprints

A fingerprint is made of a number of ridges and valleys on the surface of the finger.

Ridges are the upper skin layer segments of the finger (dark lines), and valleys are the lower segments (white spaces).

Ridges on the fingers help provide a better grip.

Why Fingerprints Are Left Behind

Fingerprints are left behind on surfaces because of these ridge patterns.

Oils from sweat glands collect on our fingers. When we touch something, a small amount of the oils and other materials on our fingers are left on the surface of the object we touched in the pattern of our ridges.

Properties That Make a Print Important

Fingerprints are considered to be unique, with no two fingers having the exact same ridge pattern characteristics.

A person's prints are consistent over his/her lifetime.

The systematic classification used for fingerprints can help identify the owner of a print of unknown origin.

Ridge Patterns as Evidence

Fingerprints are unique because each print is made up of different ridge patterns.

A print from a crime scene will be compared to known prints on file to determine who left the print.

Criminal courts generally accept 8 to 12 points of similarity as sufficient proof.

There are several types of ridge patterns as shown below. Fingerprint examiners look for these ridge patterns when comparing fingerprints.

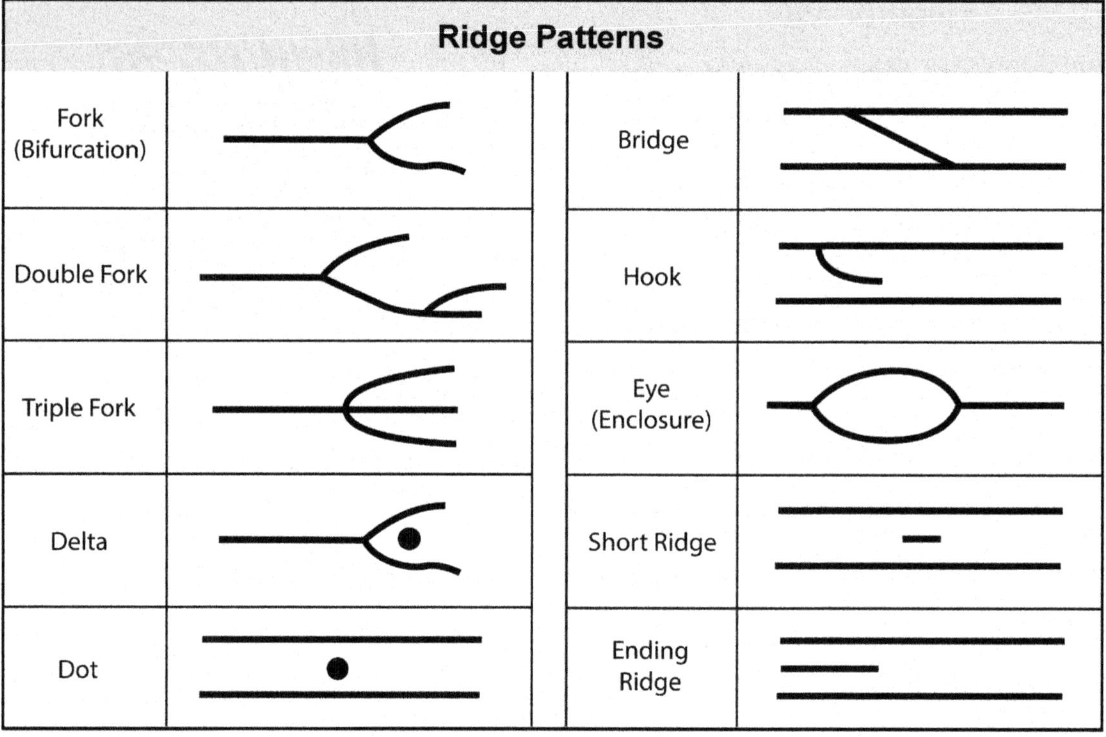

Ridge Patterns			
Fork (Bifurcation)		Bridge	
Double Fork		Hook	
Triple Fork		Eye (Enclosure)	
Delta		Short Ridge	
Dot		Ending Ridge	

Main Classifications of Fingerprints

Arch Pattern

The ridges enter from one side of the finger and exit on the other side.

Approximately 5% of all fingerprints are arches.

Loop Pattern

One or more ridges are coming from one side, curving, and then going out from the same side it entered.

Approximately 65% of all fingerprints are loops.

Whorl Pattern

Roughly circular, with the ridge lines going all the way around.

Approximately 30% of all fingerprints are whorls.

Fingerprints

Fingerprints can be found on practically any solid surface, including the human body. Some prints are easily seen, while others are invisible to the naked eye. Fingerprints are also identified by the type of surface they are found on, as well as whether or not they are visible. The three main types of fingerprints are plastic, visible and latent.

Types of Fingerprints		
Plastic Prints	**Visible Prints**	**Latent Prints**
Easily seen. Formed by pressing a finger against a soft surface (gum, putty, melted chocolate bar) and leaving a 3D print or a negative impression.	Easily seen. Formed when blood, ink, paint, grease, dust, etc. is transferred from a finger to a surface or is on a surface and is touched by a finger.	Basically invisible. Must be revealed by chemical or physical process.

Recovering Fingerprints

Often, fingerprints at a crime scene are invisible and need to be developed to make them visible for inspection and analysis.

Various methods for revealing the prints may be used depending on the surface being examined. Frequently used methods include (1) dusting, (2) using the chemical ninhydrin, and (3) superglue fuming. The method used to reveal the print will depend on the type of surface the print is on.

Dusting

One of the most common methods for revealing and collecting latent fingerprints is by dusting a smooth or nonporous surface.

Black fingerprint powder is normally used, although other powder colors do exist.

If there is a print on the surface, the powder will stick to the oils on the ridges of the fingerprint left behind.

The revealed prints are photographed. They are then covered with clear adhesive tape. The tape is lifted and then placed on a card. The card is taken to the crime lab for examination.

Ninhydrin

Porous surfaces such as paper are typically soaked or sprayed with chemicals such as ninhydrin.

This chemical reacts with the amino acids contained in the oils left behind with the print.

Applying heat, such as running a hot iron over the paper, speeds up the processing.

As a result of the reaction, the otherwise invisible prints turn a purple color.

The color makes it easy to see, photograph, and examine the now exposed print.

Superglue (Cyanoacrylate) Fuming

This process, typically performed on non-porous surfaces (metals, electrical tape, grocery bags, etc.), exposes the object to vapors.

The evidence and a touch of superglue are placed in a chamber and then heated.

The fumes and the evidence are contained within an enclosed chamber for up to 6 hours.

The vapors (fumes) will stick to any prints present on the object, producing a white appearing print.

Matching Prints

Once a fingerprint has been recovered, fingerprint examiners must determine to whom the print belongs. This is done by using a computer program called "AFIS" which stands for "Automated Fingerprint Identification System."

AFIS is a system that uses biometric technology to store digital imagery of individual fingerprints for database comparison to produce a match.

Whose Fingerprints Are Stored in AFIS?

Known criminals and identified suspects

Anyone charged with a crime

Military personnel

Police/Secret Service/FBI/firemen

Educators

Finance workers (stockbrokers, bankers)

Health care workers

Anyone needing a background check for employment

How AFIS Works

When a person is arrested their fingerprints are scanned into a database.

When a fingerprint of unknown origin is found at a crime scene, it is also scanned into AFIS.

The AFIS database picks out the most likely matches to the new print being fed into the system, narrowing the search parameters for investigators.

The comparison takes the computer only minutes to do a job, which would have otherwise taken weeks or longer for an examiner to do without the computer.

Final analysis of the print and the retrieved images is done by AFIS technicians to ensure accuracy of identification.

Foolproof Fingerprints

Fingerprints are considered a foolproof method for identification purposes because each fingerprint is unique. Recovery of fingerprints from a crime scene can play an important role in helping detectives solve cases.

CRIME SCENE REPORTS AND GENERAL FORMS

Bass Lake Police Department
Case File Introduction

Case Number: 033095 **Date:** _______________

Detectives Assigned to the Case:

____

Something's Fishy at Lake Iwannafisha. The Bass Lake Police Department was recently called to Hartmann's fishing cabin at 123 Trout Lane, to find a building in flames, a dead body, scattered bones in the woods, and stacks of money. Oh yes, throw in a couple of guns and we've got ourselves a real mystery.

You and your fellow detectives have been assigned to this case. It is your job to fully investigate this case by examining the crime scene, analyzing witness statements, and interpreting evidence. In order to see justice served, you and your team must piece together the parts of this puzzle to determine who is responsible for the crime(s) occurring at 123 Trout Lane.

Document your process by recording pertinent information in this case file. You will need to determine what path your investigation will take. When you decide what reports or statements you will need, please request them from your sergeant (teacher).

To start your investigation, you will need to read the original preliminary crime scene report, as well as see a map of the crime scene. It is up to you to use your investigative skills and forensic knowledge to crack this case.

Good Luck!

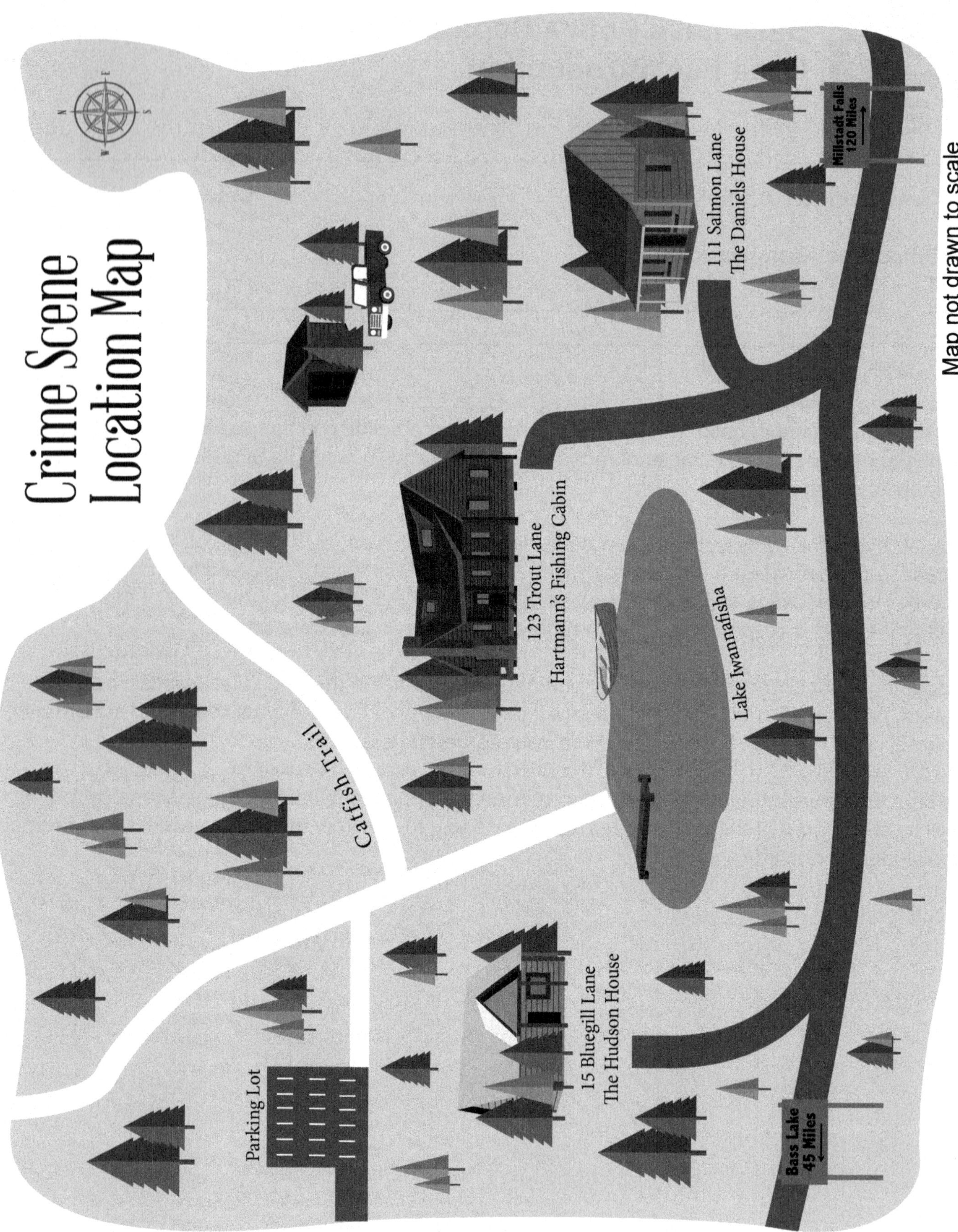
Crime Scene Location Map
123 Trout Lane
Hartmann's Fishing Cabin
111 Salmon Lane
The Daniels House
15 Bluegill Lane
The Hudson House
Lake Iwannafisha
Catfish Trail
Parking Lot
Bass Lake 45 Miles
Millstadt Falls 120 Miles
Map not drawn to scale

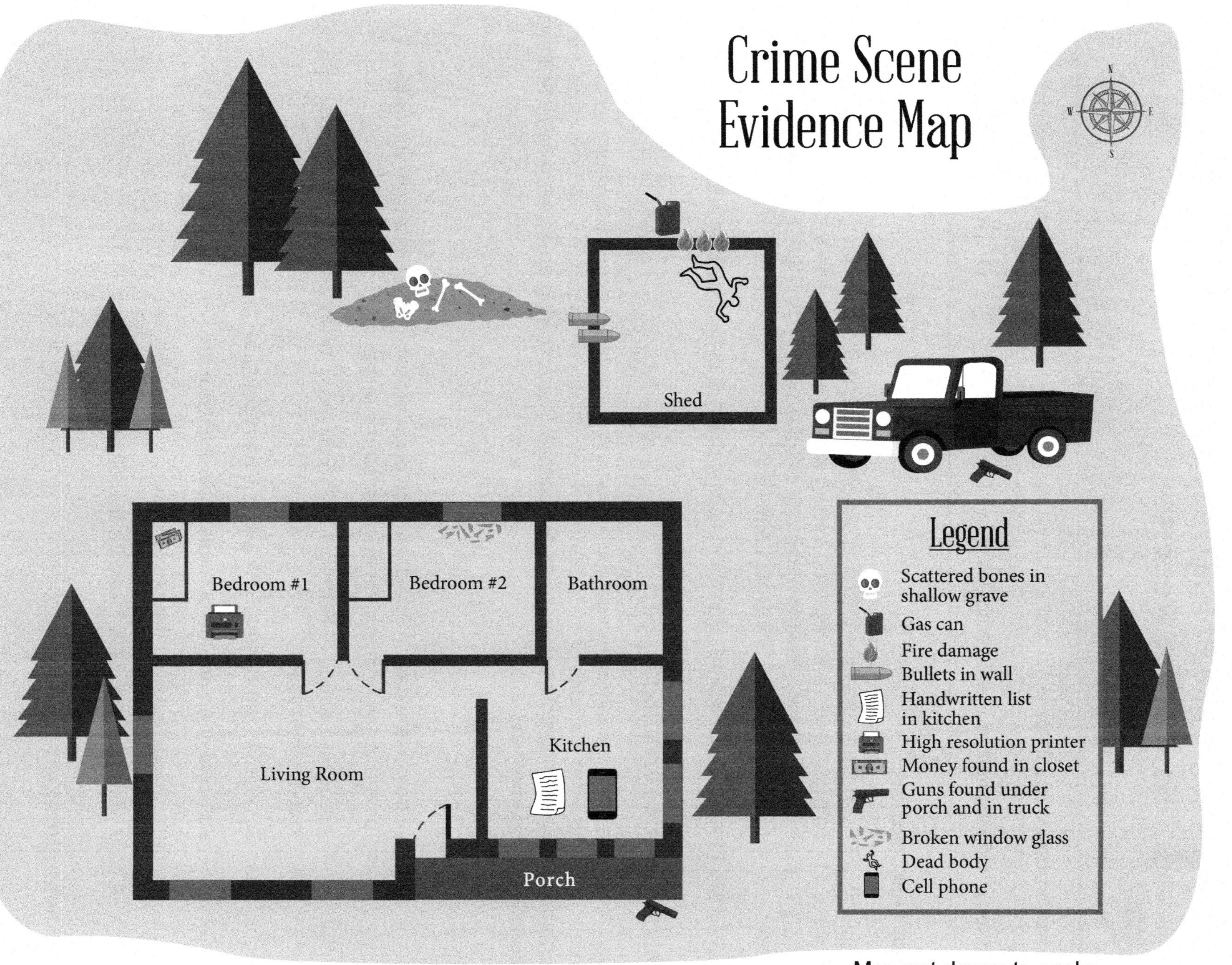
Crime Scene
Evidence Map
N
W
E
S
Shed
Bedroom #1
Bedroom #2
Bathroom
Kitchen
Living Room
Porch
Legend
Scattered bones in shallow grave
Gas can
Fire damage
Bullets in wall
Handwritten list in kitchen
High resolution printer
Money found in closet
Guns found under porch and in truck
Broken window glass
Dead body
Cell phone
Map not drawn to scale

Bass Lake Police Department
Crime Scene Report

Case Number: 033095 **Date:** June 5, 2017

Detective Assigned to the Case: Detective Jim Michaels

Case Description

On June 5, 2017, at approximately 9:45 a.m. a call was received from Taylor Daniels who resides at 111 Salmon Lane. She reported seeing smoke at a neighboring fishing cabin located at 123 Trout Lane, just on the outskirts of the city of Bass Lake. The BLPD, as well as the fire department, were dispatched to 123 Trout Lane.

City of Bass Lake property records show the fishing cabin is owned by Matthew Hartmann.

Preliminary Observations

When the police and firefighters arrived, the firemen immediately located the smoke as coming from a burning shed at the back of the property. They quickly extinguished the fire. Once the fire had been put out, the police canvassed the scene. The following areas were searched and observations documented.

The Fishing Cabin

1. One window in the back of the cabin had been broken. Glass from the window was found on the inside of one of the two bedrooms in the cabin.
2. Upon further inspection of bedroom #1, 15 stacks of twenty-dollar bills totaling $15,000 were found in the closet.
3. Also recovered from bedroom #1 was a high resolution printer.
4. Police officers discovered a gun under the front porch.
5. An iPhone was found on the kitchen table.
6. A handwritten list was also found on the kitchen table.

Lake Iwannafisha

1. A small lake lies in the front of the property.
2. A rowboat was pulled up on the bank of the lake in front of the fishing cabin.

The Shed

1. A wooden shed exists on the back of the property approximately 500 yards from the cabin. The shed, on fire when authorities arrived, was partially damaged by the fire before the fire was extinguished.
2. An empty gasoline can was found at the back of the shed.
3. An unidentified body was found dead in the shed.
4. Two bullets were found embedded in the west side wall of the shed.

Pick-Up Truck

1. On the east side of the shed, a blue Ford pick-up truck was found. The truck had no license plates. The VIN was located and was documented as C4PWR7JLW99623.
2. Keys were found in the ignition of the truck.
3. A gun was found in the glove box.

Shallow Grave

1. In the woods behind the cabin, just west of the shed, a shallow grave was discovered.
2. Four bones were found at the grave.

This concludes the preliminary crime scene report. Evidence will be collected and analyzed by the appropriate departments.

Detective Jim Michaels

Bass Lake Police Department
Case File 033095

Investigation Notes

After reading the Crime Scene Report Case 033095 submitted by Det. Jim Michaels, record your thoughts and observations below to help you plan your investigation.

1. **Criminal Action**

   Based on what was found on the property and in the cabin, list the potential crime(s) that may have taken place.

2. **Physical Evidence**

   What pieces of potential physical evidence do you see at the crime scene that you would like to further examine? Describe the evidence and give the location. Then, explain how that evidence might help you solve this case. Note: You may or may not use all of the rows in the chart.

Description of Evidence	Location Recovered	Explain How This Evidence Might Help You Solve the Case
1.		
2.		
3.		
4.		
5.		

Description of Evidence	Location Recovered	Explain How This Evidence Might Help You Solve the Case
6.		
7.		
8.		
9.		
10.		
11.		
12.		
13.		
14.		
15.		
16.		

3. **Testimonial Evidence**

What people (witnesses, neighbors, etc.) might you want to interview? List the person and describe what information you hope to gain from interviewing this person. If you don't know this person by name, then just list the relationship—neighbor, owner of cabin, etc. Note: You may or may not use all of the rows in the chart.

Persons You Want to Interview	Information You Hope to Gain
1.	
2.	
3.	
4.	
5.	
6.	
7.	
8.	
9.	
10.	

4. **Experts/Forensic Scientists**

What experts do you need to help you with this case? What evidence will they examine? How will this help you solve this case? Note: You may or may not use all of the rows in the chart.

Expert/Scientist	Evidence They May Examine and How This Might Help You Solve the Case
1.	
2.	
3.	
4.	
5.	
6.	
7.	
8.	

5. **Next Steps**

Now that you have had some time to look over and analyze this case, it is time to start investigating. Will you ask for a witness statement? Do you want to see a forensic report? As a team, determine your first plan of action and see your sergeant (teacher) with your request. As you gather information about the case, keep track of your findings on the forms provided in this case file.

Bass Lake Police Department
Case File 033095
Witness Interview Notes

As you work your way through your investigation and read each witness statement, take note of information that you think might help with the investigation. You may highlight important facts on the witness statements and then use the Witness Interview forms to summarize the most vital information.

The form has been divided into five categories as defined below. You may or may not be able to answer each question depending on the witness you are interviewing.

Categories

Connection: How is this person connected or involved with this case?

Important Facts: Record any relevant facts that you think will help the investigation move forward.

Suspicious Activity: Did this person see any suspicious activities?

Suspicions: Does this person suspect anyone? Explain who and why.

Miscellaneous Facts: Is there anything else you need to note?

Bass Lake Police Department
Case File 033095
Witness Interview Notes

Witness: ____

Connection: How is this person connected or involved with this case?
Important facts: Record any relevant facts that you think will help the investigation move forward.
Suspicious activity: Did this person see any suspicious activities? Describe what he/she saw.
Suspicions: Does this person suspect anyone? Explain who and why.
Miscellaneous facts: Is there anything else you need to note?

Bass Lake Police Department
Case File 033095
Person of Interest Profiles

As you navigate through your investigation, use the Person of Interest Profile forms to record information about each possible suspect. You may not have information to write in each of the categories. Categories are defined below.

Categories

Reason for being a suspect: Describe why you believe this person may have committed a crime, along with the crime you believe they committed.

Time frame: Where was the suspect during the supposed times the crimes were committed (time during the day, specific days, weeks, months, etc.)?

Alibi: Does this suspect have an alibi? Was this suspect with someone during the supposed times the crimes were committed?

Handwriting sample: Is a handwriting sample needed? Was it a match to the list found at the cabin?

Fingerprint samples: Are fingerprint samples needed? Did any of them match any of the prints found at the crime scene?

Vehicle ownership: Does this suspect own a vehicle that may have been involved in some way with any crimes?

Miscellaneous information: Anything else you found out that you want to record?

Summary: Do you have any final thoughts about this person of interest? Is this person your main suspect or was this person ruled out as a suspect?

Bass Lake Police Department
Case File 033095
Person of Interest Profile

Person of Interest: ______________________________

Reason for Being a Suspect	Time Frame
Alibi	Handwriting Sample
Fingerprints	Vehicle Ownership
Miscellaneous Information	Summary

Bass Lake Police Department
Missing Persons' Report

Five people have been reported missing in the area within the last 18 months. Profiles and known details for the missing persons are included in this report.

Alexa Ryan

Gender: Female
Race: Caucasian
Age: 28 years
Approximate Height: 5 feet 8 inches
Last Seen: Driving east out of the city of Bass Lake on January 14, 2016

Last Known Details: According to Jeremy Ryan, his wife, Alexa Ryan, left their home at 10:00 a.m. on January 14, 2016. She was going to run a few errands in Bass Lake and was then going to visit her mother in a neighboring town, Millstadt Falls. At 2:00 p.m., Jeremy Ryan received a phone call from Chelsea Moll, Alexa Ryan's mother, inquiring about Alexa's arrival. Alexa Ryan was due to arrive at her mother's house at approximately 12:00, but never showed up. Alexa did not contact her husband or her mother. Red light security cameras at the edge of town picked up Alexa Ryan's car traveling to the east, leaving the city limits of Bass Lake. She has not been seen since. There has been no activity on her credit cards or bank accounts, and her car has not been found. A missing person's report was filed on January 15, 2016.

Robbie Graber

Gender: Male
Race: Caucasian
Age: 30 years
Approximate Height: 6 feet 2 inches
Last Seen: Hiking the Catfish Trail on March 4, 2016

Last Known Details: According to his girlfriend, Peg Anglin, she and Robbie Graber met for breakfast at Mayme's Café at 7:30 a.m. on March 4, 2016. During breakfast, they made plans to eat dinner at her house at 6:00 p.m. that evening. At approximately 8:15 a.m., Robbie Graber left the Café, telling Peg he was going to go hiking on the Catfish Trail. He was driving his blue Ford pick-up truck at the time. At approximately 9:00 a.m., two hikers were leaving the Catfish Trail and saw Graber pull into the trail parking lot. He got out of his truck and headed towards the foot of the trail. This was the last time he was seen. When he didn't arrive at his girlfriend's house by 6:30 that evening, Peg Anglin grew concerned. She tried, but was unable to reach him by phone. She drove out to Catfish Trail, but his truck was not in the parking lot. After repeatedly calling and texting him without a response, she filed a missing person's report. Robbie Graber's whereabouts are unknown, as is the location of his Ford truck.

Brendyn Caden

Gender: Male
Race: Caucasian
Age: 21 years
Approximate Height: 5 feet 9 inches
Last Seen: In the Student Union Building at Bass Lake University on March 10, 2016

Last Known Details: According to his roommate, Danny Laufer, Brendyn Caden left their apartment at 8:30 a.m. to go to his psychology class, as he does every Monday, Wednesday, and Friday. As is his custom, Caden stopped by the Student Union to grab something for breakfast. University records confirm that Caden swiped his student ID card to make a purchase from the cafeteria at 8:45. According to his psychology professor, Brendyn Caden was not in attendance on March 10, 2016. Security cameras show Caden leaving the cafeteria and the Student Union Building. His whereabouts after leaving the building are unknown. Danny Laufer filed a missing person's report after Brendyn Caden failed to come home that evening.

Malik Monty

Gender: Male
Race: African American
Age: 24 years
Approximate Height: 5 feet 10 inches
Last Seen: At the Starbucks in Millstadt Falls on June 1, 2017

Last Known Details: Malik Monty was last seen on June 1 leaving the Starbucks café in Millstadt Falls, Missouri. Monty told the barista who was serving him that he was going to drive to the Catfish Trail between Millstadt Falls and Bass Lake to do some hiking. Security cameras show Malik leaving the Starbucks at 7:05 a.m. on June 1. It is unknown if Monty made it to Catfish Trail. His car was not found in the trail parking lot, and he was never seen again. According to his parents, Monty was a member of the U.S. Secret Service and was in town visiting them while on a short vacation. They reported him missing when he did not return home, and they were unable to contact him.

Andrew Hudson

Gender: Male
Race: African American
Age: 23 years
Approximate Height: 5 feet 10 inches
Last Seen: Fishing at Lake Iwannafisha on June 4, 2017

Last Known Details: According to Bella Hudson, Andrew's mother, she saw Andrew fishing from their rowboat on Lake Iwannafisha when she left their house at 10 a.m. on June 4. She repeatedly tried to contact him throughout the day and was unsuccessful in doing so. The row boat was found on the shore near the Hartmann fishing cabin. Andrew Hudson has not been seen since his mother saw him at 10 a.m. on June 4.

Bass Lake Police Department
Crime Scene Report

Case Number: 021394 **Date:** June 5, 2017

Reporting Officer: Officer Joseph Klipsch

Case Description

On June 5, 2017, at approximately 8:50 a.m. a call was received from the manager at the Quik Trip gas station in Bass Lake, Karen Kaye suspected that a customer paid for gasoline with counterfeit money.

Preliminary Report

Ms. Kaye provided security footage, which shows that on June 5, 2017, at approximately 8:45 a.m. a red Honda Accord pulled up to pump 4. A Caucasian woman got out of the car, and after filling up the tank of the car, proceeded to fill up a can of gasoline. She then placed the can of gasoline in the trunk of the car.

The woman in question then entered the store to pay for the gasoline. Security coverage from inside the store shows the woman paying with three $20.00 bills. She appeared to be distracted and in a hurry, repeatedly looking around the room before quickly leaving the store without waiting for her change. The manager examined the bills and marked them with a counterfeit detection pen. Meanwhile, the woman returned to her car and drove off. The security footage revealed the license plate on the car was ABC321.

The $20 bills in question were turned over to the Secret Service for further investigation.

Arrangements were made for Ms. Kaye to report to the police station to give an official statement.

This concludes the preliminary crime scene report.

Officer Joseph Klipsch

Bass Lake Police Department
Case File 021394

Investigation Notes

After reading the Quik Trip Crime Scene Report submitted by Officer Joseph Klipsch, record your thoughts and observations below to help you plan your investigation.

1. **Criminal Action**

   Based on what reportedly took place at the Quik Trip, list the potential crime(s) that may have taken place.

2. **Physical Evidence**

   What pieces of potential physical evidence do you see at the crime scene that you would like to further examine? Describe the evidence and give the location. Then explain how that evidence might help you solve this case. Note: You may or may not use all of the rows in the chart.

Description of Evidence	Location Recovered	Explain How This Evidence Might Help You Solve the Case
1.		
2.		
3.		

3. **Testimonial Evidence**

Which people might you want to interview? List the person and describe what information you hope to gain from interviewing this person. If you don't know this person by name, then just list the relationship—woman driving car, manager, etc. Note: You may or may not use all of the rows in the chart.

Persons You Want to Interview	Information You Hope to Gain
1.	
2.	
3.	

4. **Experts/Forensic Scientists**

What experts do you need to help you with this case? What evidence will they examine? How will this help you solve this case? Note: You may or may not use all of the rows in the chart.

Experts/Scientists	Evidence to Examine that May Give Information to Help You Solve the Case
1.	
2.	
3.	

5. **Next Steps**

Now that you have had some time to look over and analyze this case, it is time to start investigating. Will you ask for a witness statement? Do you want to see a forensic report? As a team, determine your first plan of action and see your sergeant (teacher) with your request. As you gather information about the case, keep track of your findings on the forms provided in this case file.

Throughout the course of your investigation, as relevant events are revealed, document the time frame of those events.

Timeline of Events 2016

January	February	March
April	May	June
July	August	September
October	November	December

Timeline of Events 2017

January	February	March
April	**May**	**June**
July	**August**	**September**
October	**November**	**December**

Bass Lake Police Department
Case Closed: Final Report
Case Numbers: 021394 and 033095

When you believe you have determined the crimes that have been committed, who committed them, and their motives, you will need to share this information with your sergeant (teacher). Complete this report to summarize your final conclusions on this case. Be very specific and detailed as you may be called on to testify in court.

1. **Main Suspect(s)**

   List who you will be charging, describe the crime with which he/she is being charged, as well as his/her motive. (Use as many rows as needed.)

Name of Person Charged	Description of Crime Committed	Description of Motive

2. **Eliminated Suspects**

During your investigation were there other people on your list of possible suspects? If so, identify them in the table below.

Eliminated Suspects	Describe the Evidence (physical or testimonial) That Allowed You to Eliminate This Person as a Suspect

3. **Victims**

Identify each of the victims found at the crime scene and describe how you identified each person. Be detailed in your justification, giving specific facts from official reports and/or witness statements.

Location of Victim	Identity of Victim (name)	Specific Facts to Support Your Conclusion
Body found in shed		
Bones found in shallow grave		

4. **Physical Evidence**

Give the relevant facts from each department report that support the reasons why you believe the identified person(s) committed the crime.

Arson: List the facts that justify the fire at the shed was arson.	**Ballistics:** Identify which guns fired which bullets, giving the location of bullets/guns.
Fingerprints: List who's fingerprints were found and where.	**Documents/Handwriting:** Tell who wrote the list and why it was important to the case.
Counterfeit Money: Describe the role this plays in the crime spree.	**Automobile Report:** Tell who owns the car seen leaving the fishing cabin and who owns the blue truck. Describe why knowing this is important.

5. **Additional Information**

As in many police investigations, some of the evidence gathered is circumstantial. And in some cases, police officers wish they had additional bits of information to help them piece together the case. Before you make your final conclusions, what additional information do you wish you had? This could be physical or testimonial evidence. Attach additional paper if needed.

List and/or Describe Additional Facts or Evidence That You Wish You Had to Help You Solve This Case	Explain Why This Will Help Solve This Case
1.	
2.	
3.	
4.	

6. **Summary of Final Conclusions**

Based on the information you recovered during your investigation, write a narrative describing the events that you believe took place leading up to the crimes. In other words, tell who, why, when (timeline) and how the crime(s) were committed. Write or type your narrative in complete sentences. Attach additional paper as needed.

Case Debriefing: Teacher Led Group Discussion

When all groups have finished with the simulation, it is a valuable use of time to discuss their course of action. It is interesting to see what path each group took and how different paths could lead to the same conclusion. Also interesting is listening to the reasoning skills they used to draw appropriate conclusions.

Here are sample discussion questions you might ask the class (not given in any particular order):

1. What was the turning point in the case? In other words, what clue (piece of evidence or witness statement) led you to your main suspects?
2. What was the link between the bones buried in the woods and the body found in the shed?
3. On June 5, Patsy Bolen was seen at the gas station in Bass Lake at 8:45. Her car was later reported to be leaving the fishing cabin at 9:45 a.m. She claimed she could not have been at the fishing cabin because she was in Bass Lake. Could she have made it from Bass Lake to the fishing cabin in an hour? How did you determine that?
4. What caused Patsy and Tyler to leave the fishing cabin so abruptly on June 5?
5. In what ways was this like a real police investigation? How was it different?
6. What, if anything, didn't make sense to you?
7. What other pieces of information or physical evidence would you have liked to have had in order to make a stronger case?
8. Were there any loose ends that you wanted resolved?
9. What piece(s) of physical evidence did you think was the most helpful in solving the case?
10. Which witness testimony did you think was most helpful in solving the case?

WITNESS STATEMENTS

Bass Lake Police Department
Witness Statement

Case Number: 033095 **Date:** June 10, 2017

Witness: Patsy Bolen

Patsy Bolen was seen at the Quik Trip gas station at Bass Lake and is suspected of paying with counterfeit money. It is also believed she is associated with Tyler Terrington. Her statement is recorded below.

1. **Please state your name.**
   Patsy Bolen
2. **Where do you live?**
   I live in Millstadt Falls.
3. **Where were you on June 5, 2017?**
   I went to Bass Lake to shop at the outlet malls.
4. **What time were you there?**
   I arrived at the mall around 8:30 a.m. and was back home by 5:00 that night.
5. **Was anyone with you?**
   No, I went by myself.
6. **Did you at any time during June 5, make a stop at the Hartmann fishing cabin, just outside of Bass Lake?**
   No.
7. **What kind of car do you drive?**
   Honda Accord
8. **What color is your car?**
   Red
9. **Did you stop for gasoline at the Quick Trip in Bass Lake?**
   Hmmm, I might have.
10. **According to security tape footage taken from the QT, you were seen getting gas at 8:45 a.m.**
    Oh, well I guess I did then.

11. **How did you pay for the gasoline?**
    I don't remember.

12. **According to security footage inside the store, you paid in cash.**
    Well, if you knew how I paid, why did you even ask?

13. **Our police department received a call from the station manager shortly after you left the station, reporting that you paid with cash that she suspected was counterfeit.**
    Okay, you got the wrong lady. I don't know anything about counterfeit money.

14. **According to our investigation, the money you used was, indeed, counterfeit.**
    Like I said, I don't know anything about that. You are mistaken.

15. **A reliable witness reported seeing your car leaving the Hartmann fishing cabin on June 5 at approximately 9:45 a.m.**
    That wasn't me. Like you just said, I was at the QT at 8:45 in the morning. No way I could have made it to the fishing cabin by 9:45.

16. **Have you ever stayed at the Hartmann fishing cabin?**
    No, I haven't.

17. **So, you didn't stay at the cabin last year between March 3 and March 14?**
    No.

18. **According to the owner, Matthew Hartmann, your car was listed as a registered guest under the name of Tyler Terrington. What is your relationship to Mr. Terrington?**
    He is my boyfriend, but I never stayed at the cabin.

19. **You weren't at the cabin with him?**
    No, but sometimes he uses my car. Maybe he was driving it then. I just don't remember. You would have to talk to him.

20. **And where is Tyler now?**
    I have no idea.

21. **Ms. Bolen, are you aware that two bodies were recently discovered at the Hartmann fishing cabin?**
    Wait, what? No, no, I don't...I didn't, what exactly are you implying?

22. **Ms. Bolen, things are not looking so good for you. Two suspected murders. A trail of counterfeit money. I think you better start talking.**
    I'm not saying another word without my lawyer!

Bass Lake Police Department
Witness Statement

Case Number: 033095 **Date:** June 5, 2017

Witness: Taylor Daniels

Taylor Daniels resides at 111 Salmon Lane, Bass Lake, Missouri. On the morning of June 5 at approximately 9:45 a.m. Ms. Daniels called 911 to report seeing and smelling smoke from a neighboring house. Her statement is recorded below.

1. **Please state your name.**
   My name is Taylor Daniels.
2. **What prompted you to call 911 on the morning of June 5?**
   I was outside in my backyard, and I smelled smoke. I turned around and I saw this thick black smoke coming from what appeared to be an area behind the fishing cabin. If I remember correctly, there is a shed behind the cabin.
3. **What time was this?**
   It was about 9:45 a.m.
4. **Did you notice if anyone was in the area of the fire?**
   Well, it wasn't exactly in the area of the fire, but I did see something unusual. Right before I made the call, I saw a red car go zooming down the road that leads away from the cabin. It startled me because I didn't think anyone was at the cabin. It was supposed to be closed for a month.
5. **Did you happen to get the make or model of the car or perhaps the license plate?**
   The car was driving by so quickly that I only caught the last three numbers of the license plate. They were 321. But I did notice it had a big dent in the driver's side back door.
6. **Did you see who was in the car?**
   There were two people in the car, but I didn't get a good look at them. I wouldn't be able to identify them.
7. **Have you ever seen this car before?**
   No, I haven't. Well, wait a minute. Give me a minute...now that I think about it, I seem to recall that there was a red car like that at the cabin last year. In the spring, I think. I remember seeing a big dent in the back door of that car too. Since the road to the cabin goes by my house and it doesn't get a lot of traffic, I tend to notice things like that. Yes, I'm sure of it. The car I saw today was the same car that was here last year.

8. **Did you notice when the car arrived at the cabin?**
   No, I didn't, but I'm thinking someone was there yesterday.

9. **Yesterday, as in June 4?**
   Yes, that's right.

10. **What makes you think someone was at the cabin yesterday?**
    Well, I was in my house eating lunch while watching TV, when I heard multiple popping noises. POP! POP! POP! It sounded like a gun was being shot, which really surprised me, as this is a no hunting area. It sounded like it was coming from back in the woods, beyond Hartmann's fishing cabin.

11. **What did you do?**
    I looked out my back door, but I didn't see anything. I waited a few more minutes to see if I could hear anything else, and I didn't, so I just went back to eating lunch and watching my TV program, *Fixer Upper*. You know, the one with Chip and Joanna Gaines, and they fix up houses. I just love that show.

12. **What time was this?**
    Let's see, it was halfway through the *Fixer Upper* show, and I was eating lunch, so it must have been around 12:30. Yes, I'm sure it was 12:30, give or take a few minutes.

13. **Did you notice anyone going to or leaving the cabin on June 4?**
    No, I didn't. But later that night, I could faintly see some lights on at the cabin. I thought perhaps Matthew, the owner of the cabin, was staying there, although he usually stops by on his way to the cabin to say hello and to let me know he is there. He didn't do that, but maybe he was just in a hurry. I'm not sure.

14. **Is there anything else you can think of that might help us with our investigation?**
    No, I can't think of anything else, but if I do I'll give you a call.

Bass Lake Police Department Witness Statement

Case Number: 033095	**Date:** June 5, 2017
Witness: Matthew Hartmann	

Matthew Hartmann is the owner of the Hartmann fishing cabin located at 123 Trout Lane in Bass Lake, Missouri. He was contacted and interviewed after the crime scene involving his property was processed. His statement is recorded below.

1. **Please state your name.**
   Matthew Hartmann
2. **Please describe the property that you own.**
   I own a fishing cabin just outside the city limits of Bass Lake. The address is 123 Trout Lane.
3. **Are you the only one currently residing at this cabin?**
   No, I only live there periodically throughout the year. It is not my main residence, but rather I use it as a vacation home. When I am not using it, I try to rent it out to help supplement my income.
4. **Were you living in the cabin at the time of the fire?**
   No, I was not.
5. **Were you renting it to anyone now?**
   No, it was not currently rented. I wanted to do some work on it, so I did not rent it between May 10 and June 10. I did finish up the work by June 1, so it has been sitting empty since then.
6. **If someone was interested in renting your cabin, how would she/he go about doing that?**
   Well, I placed an advertisement in a couple of fishing and hunting magazines. In addition, I also have a website. If someone was interested in renting the property, they could contact me through my website.
7. **Could someone just find out about your place by simply driving by?**
   Probably not. The cabin sits off the road and it is a bit isolated. Most people like the privacy it provides.
8. **When was the last time you were at the cabin?**
   I was there working on it between May 10 and June 1.
9. **And where were you between June 1 and June 5?**
   I returned to my home in Millstadt Falls. I had to go back to work.

10. **What was the condition of the cabin when you left?**
Well, it was in really good condition. I had just finished with some renovations and was in the process of bringing back the furniture. The kitchen was completed, but my plan was to furnish the bedrooms next week.

11. **When we searched the area we discovered a window in the back of the cabin was broken. Were you aware of that?**
No, I wasn't. When I left the cabin it was definitely not broken.

12. **So the cabin only had kitchen furnishings? No TVs, computers, or printers?**
Yes sir, only the kitchen was done. I had yet to move in any electronics.

13. **Well Mr. Hartmann, it appears as if someone had broken into your cabin and made themselves at home.**
What do you mean?

14. **When we searched the house we did find a phone on the kitchen table, and a high resolution printer in one of the bedrooms. Does the phone or printer belong to you?**
No, they do not.

15. **Mr. Hartmann, are you aware that stacks of $20 bills totaling $15,000 were recovered from the same bedroom that the printer was in?**
No way! You've got to be kidding me! What is going on here?

16. **That's what we would like to know. We have a few more questions for you. Did you happen to walk through the back of the property or go into the shed while you were there?**
I didn't go through the woods, but I did go into the shed where I store some tools. I didn't see anything out of place though.

17. **A blue Ford pick-up truck was found on the property next to the shed. Does this truck belong to you?**
No, it does not.

18. **Do you know who owns the truck?**
No, I don't.

19. **Do you own any guns?**
No, I do not.

20. **A gun was found under the front porch of the cabin and one was also found in the truck. Do you know who might own those guns?**
Seriously, you found a gun under the porch? Okay, this is getting scary. No, I don't know who they belong to or how they got there.

21. **Is the boat on the shore yours?**
No.

22. **Any idea who the owner of the boat might be?**
Well, it might be the neighbor's. I think his name is Andrew something. He lives across the lake. I've seen him out in a boat similar to that but since I'm not here that often I don't know him that well.

23. **At the time the fire was being reported a red car was seen driving down the road away from the cabin. Do you know to whom the car might belong?**
I have no clue.

24. **The neighbor who lives at 111 Salmon Lane said she thought the car was the same as one she saw last year at the cabin. She said both cars had the same dent in them. Do you remember to whom you rented the place?**
I'll have to go through my records. Business was slow last winter so I didn't rent it out too many times. I've got access to my records on my phone, let me check real quick. Here is it, in the winter/spring of 2016 it looks like it was rented from January 1 to January 7, from February 22 through March 2, and from March 3 to March 14.

25. **Who did you rent it to during those days?**
From January 1 to January 7 it was rented to Cheryl Young. From February 22 to March 2 my uncle Mike Hartmann rented it and from March 3 to March 14 Tyler Terrington rented it.

26. **Did any of those people drive a red car?**
I don't know what color the cars were. In each case, I just left the keys under door mat and they let themselves in. As part of their registration, I did get the make and model of their car along with their license plate number. I can look up those records for you if you think it might help.

27. **That would be very helpful.**
Okay here they are: Cheryl Young drives a Kia Optima, license plate number CLH608. Mike Hartmann drives a Ford truck, license plate number HFS128, and Tyler Terrington drives a Honda Accord, license plate number ABC321.

28. **Is there anyone you can think of who is angry with you or would want to take revenge on you?**
No, I can't think of anyone. I'm a pretty likable guy; I can get along with anyone.

29. **Sir, we would like to get a record of your fingerprints so we can distinguish yours from any other prints we might uncover during the investigation.**
Yes, absolutely. I want to do everything I can to help you figure out what is going on.

30. **Thank you for your time today, Mr. Hartmann. If you think of any other information that might help with this case, no matter how trivial, please don't hesitate to contact us.**

Bass Lake Police Department Witness Statement

Case Number: 033095 **Date:** June 7, 2017

Witness: Michael Hartmann

According to Matthew Hartmann, Michael Hartmann rented the Hartmann fishing cabin from February 22 to March 2, 2016. Michael Hartmann's statement is recorded below.

1. **Please state your name.**
   Mike Hartmann
2. **Where do you live?**
   I'm from Millstadt Falls.
3. **Where were you between February 22 and March 2, 2016?**
   I was vacationing at my nephew's fishing cabin.
4. **Was anyone else with you?**
   My daughters, Emily and Jessica were with me.
5. **Did you see anyone hiking in the woods or on Catfish Trail during your stay?**
   No, I did not. But we did spend most of our time fishing.
6. **What vehicle do you drive?**
   I drive a Ford Truck. Well, I did drive a Ford Truck. It was stolen a couple of weeks ago. It hasn't been found yet.
7. **What color is the truck and what is the license plate number?**
   Blue and the plate number is HFS128
8. **Where were you between June 1 and June 5 of this year?**
   Let me think. During the day I was at work at my business, Hartmann Farm Supply, and during the evenings I was at home with my girls, Emily and Jessica.
9. **Is there anyone who can confirm this?**
   My employees at Hartmann Farm Supply can confirm this. You could also ask Emily and Jessica. They were home with me in the evenings.*

10. **Sir, would you be willing to be fingerprinted to assist us in further investigating this crime scene.**

    Sure, I've got nothing to hide.

11. **Thank you. At this time, we have no further questions.**

*Note: On June 8, 2017, employees at Hartmann Farm Supply were questioned and confirmed that Mike Hartmann was at his place of business between June 1 and June 5. In addition, his daughters Emily and Jessica confirmed his presence at his home in Millstadt Falls during the questioned time period.

Bass Lake Police Department
Witness Statement

Case Number: 033095 **Date:** June 5, 2017

Witness: Bella Hudson

Bella Hudson, the mother of Andrew Hudson, resides with her son at 15 Bluegill Lane. She reported her son missing on June 5, 2017. Her statement is recorded below.

1. **Please state your name.**
   Bella Hudson
2. **How are you related to Andrew Hudson.**
   I am his mother.
3. **And you are here today to file a missing person's report?**
   That is correct. I am afraid something terrible has happened to my son.
4. **When is the last time you saw your son?**
   It was yesterday, June 4. I had made Andrew some eggs and bacon for breakfast around 9:00 that morning. Shortly after that I left to go out of town for a few days to visit my sister. I was pulling out of the driveway around 10 a.m. when I saw him in our rowboat out on Lake Iwannafisha. Andrew teaches at the local high school and school was out for the summer. He was excited about kicking the summer off by doing a little fishing. I waved good-bye and that was the last time I saw him.
5. **Did you try making contact with your son that day?**
   Oh, yes. I called him when I got to my sister's house around 12 p.m., but he didn't answer his phone.
6. **Is it unusual that he didn't answer his phone?**
   No, not really. I mean I knew he was probably still fishing, but what was unusual was that he never called me back. He always calls me back at some point in time.
7. **How many times did you try to contact him yesterday, June 4?**
   Three or four times. Right after I called him, I also texted him. I told him to either call or text me. I called again at 2:00, 5:00, and again at 9:00 that night, but still no answer. That is when I really started to worry.

8. **Did you try contacting him again today, June 5?**

   Yes, I did. I called as soon as I got up around 8:00 in the morning and finally I texted him at 9:00 a.m. I told him I was giving him 30 minutes, and if he didn't call or text back, I was calling the police.

9. **And did he call or text?**

   No, he did not.

10. **So then, after 30 minutes, you decided to call the police?**

    Yes, it was about 9:30 a.m. when I called the Bass Lake police. They told me they would be sending a patrol car to check out my house and the surrounding area. I texted my son one last time around 9:30 and told him the police were on their way. The fact that he never responded really frightened me. I just know something happened to him. After calling the police, I left my sister's house immediately to come home.

11. **Did you see anything unusual at home?**

    No, I arrived at my house around 11:45 and everything seemed to be in order. I did notice our fishing boat was no longer at our dock.

12. **What did you do next?**

    I looked around the house and our property, but there was no sign of him. I didn't know what to do, so I drove to the police station to speak to someone in person about my son.

13. **Is there anything else you can think of? Anywhere your son could have gone or anyone he would be with?**

    No, there isn't. As I said, my son is a teacher, and I know he was looking forward to starting his summer by hanging out at home and just doing some fishing. If he had a change of plans I know he would have told me.

14. **Thanks for your time ma'am. If you think of anything else or hear from your son, please contact us immediately. We will continue searching for him and we'll keep you posted on our progress.**

Bass Lake Police Department
Witness Statement

Case Number: 021394 **Date:** June 5, 2017

Witness: Karen Kaye

Karen Kaye is the manager of the Quik Trip gas station in Bass Lake. She called 911 to report she suspected counterfeit money was used to pay for gasoline. Her statement is recorded below.

1. **Please state your name.**
   My name is Karen Kaye.
2. **Where were you on this morning?**
   I was at work. I am the manager of the Quik Trip gas station in Bass Lake.
3. **According to our records you called the police around 8:50 a.m. Is that correct?**
   Yes, that's right.
4. **What prompted you to call the police?**
   I thought a customer paid for her gasoline with counterfeit money.
5. **What made you think the money was counterfeit?**
   All employees of Quik Trip are trained in detecting counterfeit money. When I was holding the money I noticed it didn't feel like regular money. I used a counterfeit detection pen to test it out and sure enough it left a black mark on all three bills. Also, when I held it up to the light I did not see a watermark.
6. **Did you try to detain the customer?**
   No, I didn't even have a chance. She handed me the money and then just left. She didn't even wait for her change. She was acting really strange the whole time.
7. **Would you please describe her "strange" behavior?**
   Well, when she walked up to the check-out counter to pay she just kept looking down and she wouldn't make eye contact with me. Most customers are really friendly and talkative, but not this lady. She didn't say a word. She appeared to be distracted and in a hurry, repeatedly looking around the room. She handed me her money and then quickly left the store without waiting for her change.

8. **What kind of car was she driving?**
   I'm not sure of the make or model but it was a 4-door red car. I remember the car pulling in because it had this big dent on the back section of the driver's side of the car.

9. **Did you see the license plate number?**
   Yes, I did. It was ABC321.

10. **Is there anyone else who may have witnessed this interaction?**
    I don't think so. I was the only one working up front and I don't think there were any other cars getting gas at the time. I do have security cameras both inside and outside of the station. You are welcome to look at the footage from those cameras.*

11. **Thank you very much for your time. We will let you know how our investigation is going. If you think of anything else, please let us know.**

*Note: Security tapes from the Quik Trip gas station were viewed. Observations are documented on the Crime Scene Report for Case Number 021394 dated June 5, 2017.

Bass Lake Police Department
Witness Statement

Case Number: 033095 **Date:** June 10, 2017

Witness: Cheryl Young

According to Matthew Hartmann, Cheryl Young rented the Hartmann fishing cabin from January 1 to January 7, 2016. Cheryl Young's statement is recorded below.

1. **Please state your name.**
   Cheryl Young
2. **Where do you live?**
   Baldwin, Illinois
3. **Where were you between January 1 and January 7, 2016?**
   My husband Todd and I spent a week at the Hartmann fishing cabin outside of Bass Lake.
4. **Was anyone else with you?**
   No, it was just Todd and I. We own a business and had a very hectic holiday season so it was just nice to get away.
5. **What vehicle do you drive?**
   I drive a Kia Optima.
6. **What color is your car?**
   Red
7. **What is the license plate number?**
   CLH608
8. **Does your car have any damage to the body?**
   No, it is in perfect condition, not even a scratch.
9. **A reliable witness claims to have seen a red car driving away from the cabin on June 5, just a week ago. They believe it is the same car they saw in 2016. Were you at the cabin between June 1 and June 5 of this year, 2017?**
   No, we weren't. We were only at the fishing cabin one time and that was in 2016. June is a popular wedding month and we were busy working at our business, Vintage Events and Weddings. There is no way we could have left our business during that time.

10. **Is there anyone who can confirm this?**
    Our employees can confirm this.*

11. **Would you and your husband be willing to be fingerprinted in order to help us further in our investigation?**
    I'm not sure how that will help you but, yes, we can do that.

12. **Well, if we find any prints at the cabin we can rule out your prints therefore narrowing down the field of unknown prints.**
    Is your husband Todd available for questioning?

    No, he is out of town, but I don't think he would have any information to share with you that I haven't already told you.

13. **Well, thanks for speaking with us today. At this time, we have no further questions.**

*Note: On June 12, 2017, employees at Young's business, Vintage Events and Weddings, were questioned and confirmed that both Cheryl and Todd Young were at their place of business between June 1 and June 5.

FORENSIC LAB REPORTS

Bass Lake Anthropology Department

Case Number: 033095 **Preliminary Report**

Case Description: Human bones were recovered from a shallow grave in the woods on the property of 123 Trout Lane in Bass Lake, Missouri. Two of the bones were identified as a humerus and a tibia. Also recovered were a pelvic bone and a skull.

After an initial examination, the preliminary findings/observations are listed below.

1. Pelvic Bone

Narrow, long sacrum

2. Skull

A gunshot wound was found going through the front of the skull. Other findings:

Chin:	squared, U-shaped
Brow ridge:	large, prominent and heavy, sloping forehead
Cranial length:	long
Cranial breadth:	narrow
Nasal aperture:	narrow
Eye openings:	square
Eye orbits:	sloping
Sagittal sutures:	completely closed

3. Humerus bone

An arm bone measuring approximately 38.6 cm long

4. Tibia bone

A leg bone measuring approximately 45 cm long

Note: Preliminary DNA testing suggests all bones belong to the same person, however, conclusive reports are pending.

Bass Lake Anthropology Department

Case Number: 033095

Final Report

You are the Senior Anthropologist on staff at the lab. Based on the preliminary findings, what conclusions can you draw? Record your conclusions here and be sure to tell how/why (justify) you arrived at your conclusions. Be specific in your explanations should you be called to give expert testimony in court.

After examining the bones, the following conclusions can be made.

Pelvic Bone	Belonged to a: Gender: _____ male _____ female	Justification/How do you know? (be specific)
Skull	Belonged to a: Gender: _____ male _____ female Race: _____ Caucasoid _____ Negroid _____ Mongoloid Approx. age ___________	Justification/How do you know? (be specific)

Case Number: 033095

Final Report (Page 2)

Humerus Bone (38.6 cm long)	Approximately how tall (in feet and inches) is the person to whom this bone belongs? ______ ft ______ in.	Justification/How do you know? (be specific)
Tibia Bone (45 cm long)	Approximately how tall (in feet and inches) is the person to whom this bone belongs? _______ ft _____ in.	Justification/How do you know? (be specific)

Final Conclusion: You will need to prepare a statement for the lead detective in this case. Describe the person to whom you believe the bones belong giving the gender, race, age, and approximate height. Write your profile in a sentence. (For example, "The bones belong to a ....")

Bass Lake
Department of Arson Investigations

Case Number: 033095 **Preliminary Report**

Case Description: The Bass Lake Department of Arson Investigations was called to 123 Trout Lane on June 5, 2017. At approximately 9:45 a.m. Taylor Daniels, a neighbor, reported seeing smoke coming from the property.

Summary of Initial Findings

First responders who arrived on the scene noted the following:

1. A shed at the back of the property was on fire and was quickly extinguished.
2. A "V" burn pattern was found at the back of the shed, starting at the ground and spreading up the back wall.
3. The smoke coming from the shed was thick and black.
4. Flame color was reported to be a yellowish-white.
5. Copper wires in the shed were melted.
6. Windows in the shed contained small cracks/crazing.
7. An empty gasoline can was found outside at the back of the shed.
8. A deceased body was found in the shed.

Bass Lake
Department of Arson Investigations

Case Number: 033095 **Final Report**

You are the Senior Investigator on staff at the Department of Arson Investigations. Based on the preliminary report, what conclusions can you draw? Record them here and be sure to tell how/ why (justify) you arrived at your conclusions. Be specific in your explanations should you be called to give expert testimony in court.

1. Where was the origin of the fire? Explain how you arrived at your conclusion.

2. What conclusion can you draw based on the color of the smoke? Be specific.

3. What conclusion can you draw from observing the color of the flame? Be specific.

4. What conclusion can you draw from finding the presence of crazing on the windows in the shed? Be specific.

5. Copper wires were melted during the fire. What does this indicate? Be specific.

6. How does knowing the temperature at which the fire was burning help you determine whether or not the fire was accidental or an act of arson? Be specific.

Final Conclusion: You will need to prepare a statement for the lead detective in this case. In your professional opinion, was this an act of arson or an accidental fire? Justify your answer using information reported on the preliminary report. Be very detailed in your justification, giving at least 4 reasons to support your claim. Write your statement in paragraph form.

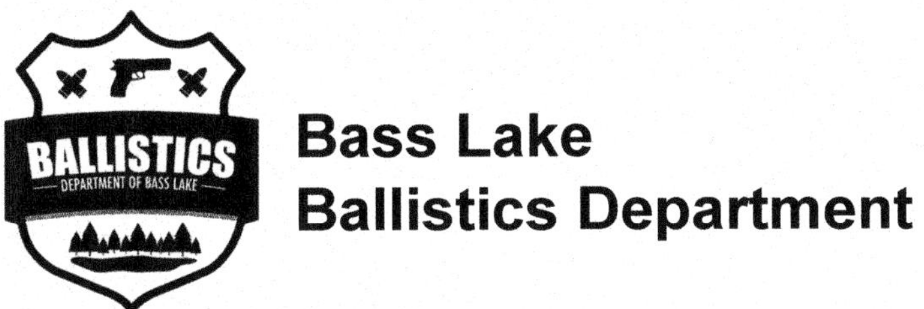

Bass Lake Ballistics Department

Case Number: 033095 **Preliminary Report** (part 1)

Case Description: On June 5, 2017, the Bass Lake Crime Scene Investigators were called to a crime scene located at the Hartmann fishing cabin at 123 Trout Lane. While investigating the scene they recovered four bullets and two guns from the area surrounding the cabin.

Summary of Initial Findings

Bullets: Four bullets were recovered from the scene.

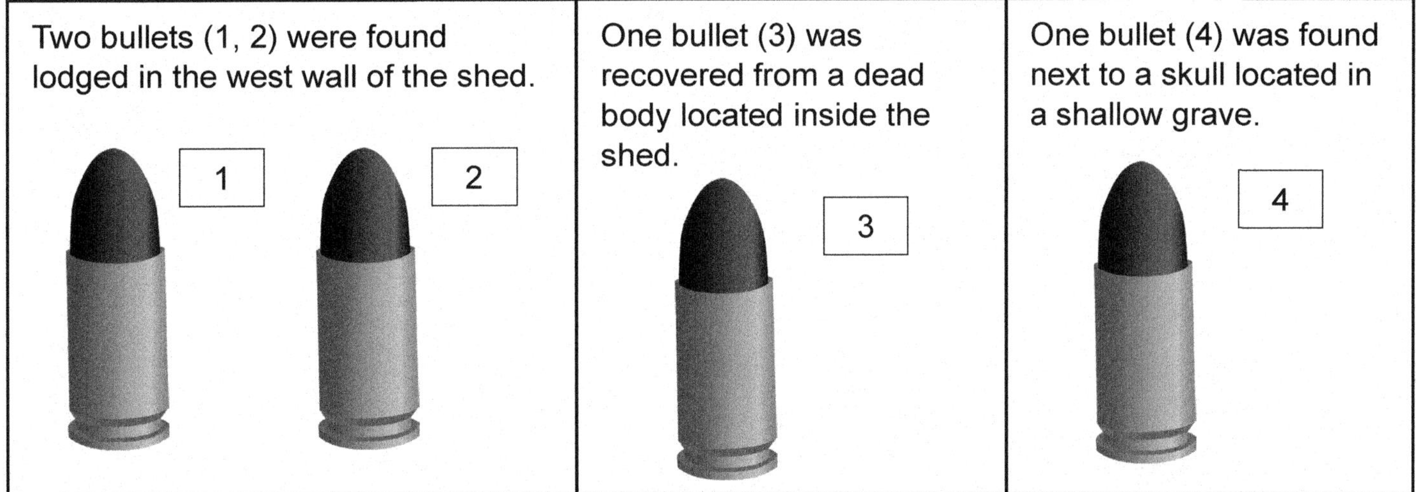

Two bullets (1, 2) were found lodged in the west wall of the shed.	One bullet (3) was recovered from a dead body located inside the shed.	One bullet (4) was found next to a skull located in a shallow grave.

Each bullet was examined and unique striations were noted and photographed.

Firearms: Two firearms were recovered from the scene.

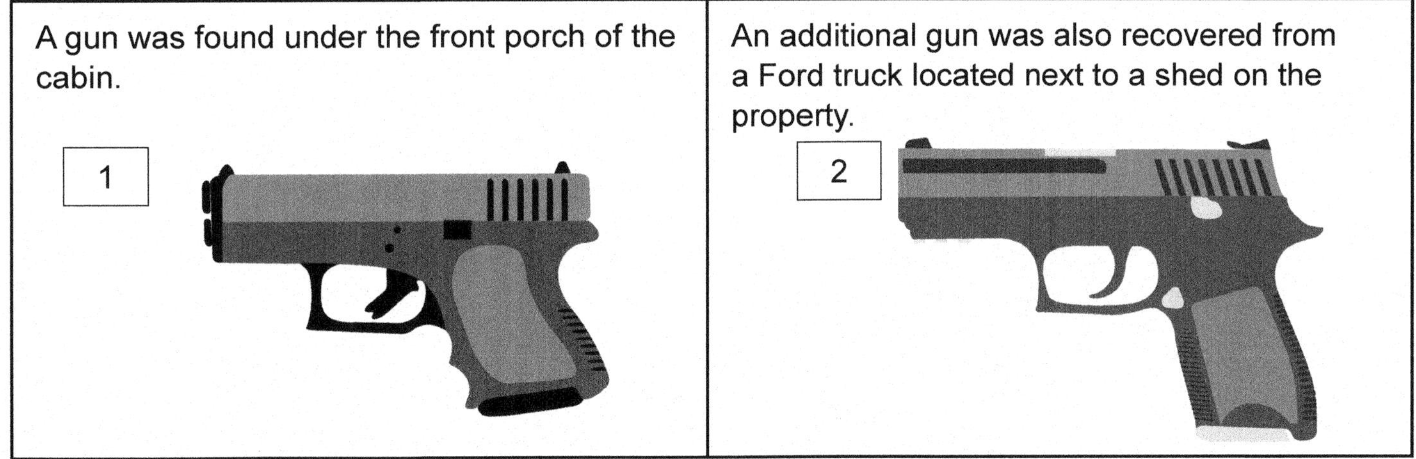

A gun was found under the front porch of the cabin.	An additional gun was also recovered from a Ford truck located next to a shed on the property.

Test bullets were fired through both guns. Unique striations were noted and photographed.

Bass Lake
Ballistics Department

Case Number: 033095 **Final Report** (part 1)

As the Senior Ballistic Analyst on staff at the lab you will need to carefully examine the bullets and guns recovered from the crime scene as well as the Ballistic Firearms and Bullets Identification Catalogs. Use this information to:

1. Determine the make of each gun that was recovered.
2. Identify the type of bullets that were recovered.

Firearms

Write the make of the guns recovered from the scene.

Gun 1: Recovered from under the front porch Make: ____________________

Gun 2: Recovered from the Ford truck Make: ____________________

Bullets

Write the caliber of the bullets recovered from each location.

Bullet 1: West wall of shed Caliber: ____________________

Bullet 2: West wall of shed Caliber: ____________________

Bullet 3: Dead body in shed Caliber: ____________________

Bullet 4: In shallow grave Caliber: ____________________

Now that you have determined the make of the guns and the type of bullets that were recovered, you must determine which gun fired which bullet.

Ask for the following reports:

Firearms Report #1 (part 2)
Firearms Report #2 (part 2)
Striations Report #1 (part 2)
Striations Report #2 (part 2)
Striations Report #3 (part 2)

Carefully read through these reports and based on your observations of the various striations, indicate which gun fired which bullet by completing the chart below.

Number and Location of Bullet	Gun That Fired This Bullet (identify by make)
Bullet 1 (embedded in west wall of shed)	
Bullet 2 (embedded in west wall of shed)	
Bullet 3 (dead body in shed)	
Bullet 4 (shallow grave)	

Final Conclusion: You will need to prepare a statement for the lead detective in this case, summarizing your findings after inspecting all guns and bullets associated with this case. Write your summary in paragraph form, describing which gun fired which bullet. Include the location from which the bullet was recovered.

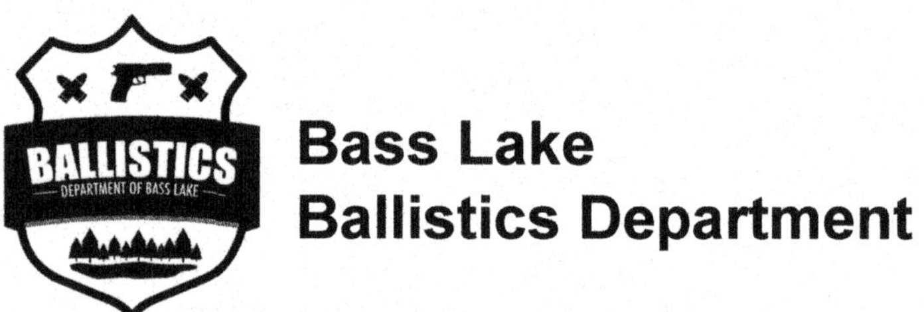

Bass Lake Ballistics Department

Firearms Identification Catalog (part 1)

Glock 26 	Ruger 
Smith and Wesson 	SIG P250 

Bass Lake Ballistics Department

Bullets Identification Catalog (part 1)

.22 caliber	9mm	.357 caliber	.40 caliber
.44 caliber	.45 caliber	.223	.300

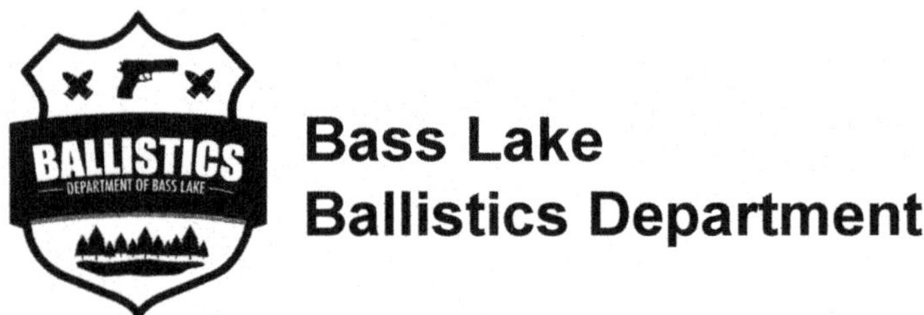

Bass Lake Ballistics Department

Case Number: 033095

Firearms Report #1 (part 2)

A **GLOCK 26** firearm was found under the front porch of the cabin. This gun uses 9mm bullets.

After examining the weapon for fingerprints and ensuring it was safe to be discharged, a test-fire of the weapon was completed. Striations found on the test bullet were noted and photographed.

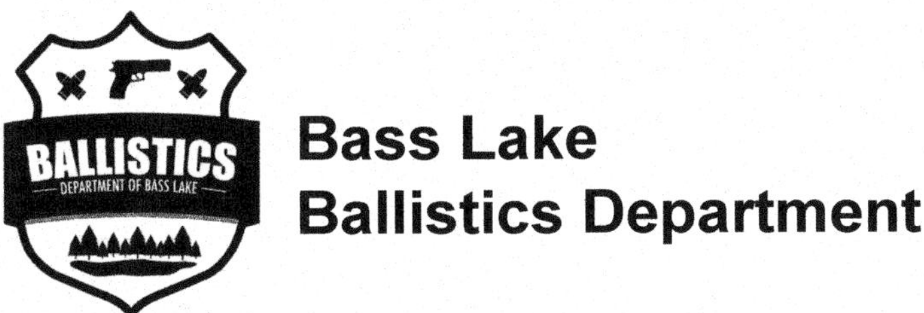

Bass Lake Ballistics Department

Case Number: 033095 **Firearms Report #2** (part 2)

A **Sig P250** firearm was found in a Ford truck that was located on the property. This gun uses 9mm bullets.

After examining the weapon for fingerprints and ensuring it was safe to be discharged, a test-fire of the weapon was completed. Striations found on the test bullet were noted and photographed.

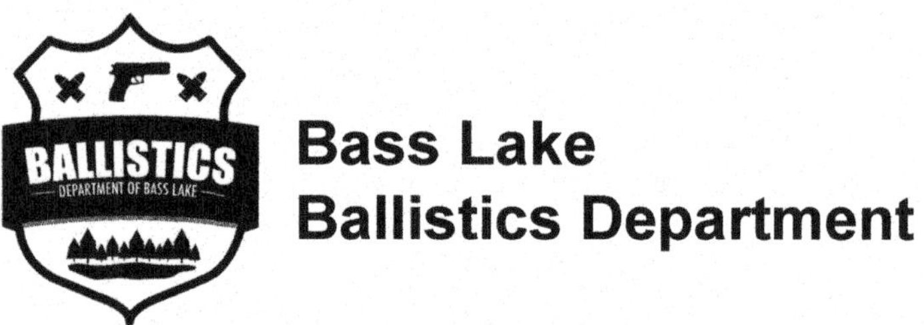

Bass Lake Ballistics Department

Case Number: 033095 **Striations Report #1** (part 2)

Two bullets were found embedded in the west side of shed. Both bullets were examined and identified as 9mm. The following striations on the bullets were noted and photographed.

Bullet 1

Bullet 2

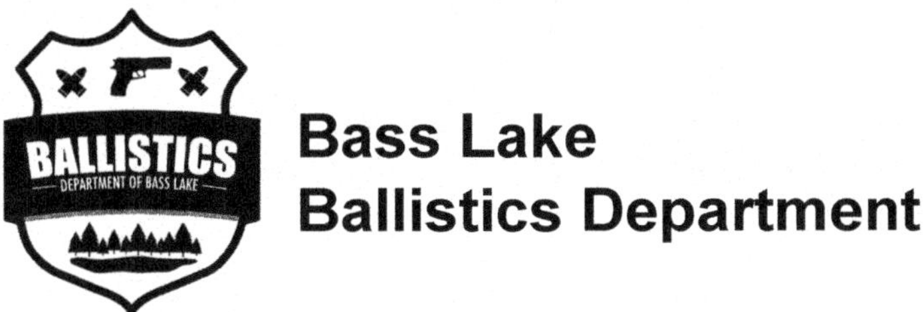

Bass Lake Ballistics Department

Case Number: 033095 **Striations Report #2** (part 2)

One bullet was recovered from the unidentified dead body found in the partially burned shed. The bullet was examined and identified as a 9mm. The following striations on the bullet were noted and photographed.

Bullet 3

Bass Lake Ballistics Department

Case Number: 033095 **Striations Report #3** (part 2)

One bullet was recovered from a shallow grave among bones of an unidentified victim. The bullet was examined and identified as a 9mm. The following striations were noted and photographed.

Bullet 4

U.S. Secret Service
Counterfeit Currency Division

Case Number: 021394 **Preliminary Report**

Case Description

On June 5, 2017, at approximately 8:50 a.m., Karen Kaye, the manager at the Quik Trip gas station in Bass Lake, phoned the Bass Lake Police Department. Ms. Kaye suspected that a customer paid for gasoline with counterfeit money. The local police department confiscated the money and turned it over to the Secret Service. The bills were examined at the Secret Service crime lab.

Summary of Initial Findings

1. Three $20 bills were confiscated upon suspicion of being counterfeit.
2. When a counterfeit detection pen was applied to the currency a black mark was left behind on the bill.
3. No randomly disbursed red and blue fibers were found to be imbedded throughout the bill.
4. The face of Andrew Jackson appeared on the bill.
5. No watermark appeared on the bill.
6. The 20 at the lower left of the bill remained a solid color. It did not change colors when shifted.
7. When placed under a UV light source, no 3D security ribbon was evident.
8. No evidence of micro-printing on the bill was found.

Conclusion: Based on the information given above, the money is (check one):

_____ **counterfeit** _____ **real**

Share your conclusion with your sergeant (teacher) and ask for the Counterfeit Currency Division Final Report handout for Case Number 021394.

U.S. Secret Service Counterfeit Currency Division

Case Number: 021394 **Final Report**

You are the Senior Special Agent who examined the questioned currency in Case Number 021394. You must share your professional opinions with the lead detective on the case. Answering the questions below will assist you in explaining how you arrived at your conclusion that the money was counterfeit. Be specific in your explanations should you be called upon to give expert testimony in court.

1. The counterfeit detection pen left a black mark on the bills that were examined. Explain why that happens when marking counterfeit money.

2. Your investigation revealed there was no watermark on the bill. In a real $20 bill, what should the watermark look like?

3. The 20 at the lower left of the bill remained a solid color when the bill was shifted. What should have happened when the bill was shifted?

4. There was no evidence of a security thread when the bill was exposed to UV light. What color of security thread should have been on the bill?

5. When examined, no clear micro-printing was found. Give two examples of where you would expect to see micro-printing on a $20 bill, as well as what it should say.

U.S. Secret Service Counterfeit Currency Division

Case Number: 033095

Preliminary Report

Case Description

On June 5, 2017, the Bass Lake Police Department was called to the Hartmann fishing cabin at 123 Trout Lane. Suspected counterfeit money was recovered by the Bass Lake Police Department and was turned over to the Secret Service. The bills were taken to the Secret Service lab and examined.

Summary of Findings

1. 15 stacks of $20 bills totaling $15,000 were confiscated.
2. When a counterfeit detection pen was applied to the currency, a yellowish mark was left behind on the bill.
3. Small randomly disbursed red and blue fibers were found to be imbedded throughout the bill.
4. The face of Andrew Jackson appeared on the bill.
5. No watermark appeared on the bill.
6. The 20 at the lower left of the bill remained a solid color when the bill was shifted.
7. When placed under a UV light source, no 3D security ribbon was evident.
8. No evidence of micro-printing on the bill was found.
9. A high resolution printer was found in the same bedroom as the currency.
10. A handwritten list containing the following words was also recovered:

Dish Pan
Gloves
Measuring Cup (ml)
Printer
Paper
CH3COCH3
NaClO
$1 bills

Conclusion: Based on the information given above, the money is (check one):

_____ **counterfeit**

_____ **real**

Share your conclusion with your sergeant (teacher) and ask for the Counterfeit Currency Division Final Report handout for Case Number 033095.

U.S. Secret Service Counterfeit Currency Division

Case Number: 033095 **Final Report**

You are the Senior Special Agent who examined the currency in Case Number 033095. You must share your professional opinions with the lead detective on the case. Answering the questions below will assist you in explaining how you arrived at your conclusion that the money in both cases was counterfeit. Be specific in your explanations should you be called upon to give expert testimony in court.

1. The counterfeit detection pen left a yellowish mark on the bill but yet you determined the bill to be counterfeit. Explain how this is possible.

2. The bill contained embedded red and blue fibers consistent with real money, but yet you determined the bill to be counterfeit. Explain how this is possible.

3. Your investigation revealed there was no watermark on the bill. If the counterfeiters did indeed bleach a bill and then print on top of it, what denomination did they use? Explain how you know.

4. A handwritten list was also recovered from the crime scene. After reading the contents of this list you determined that it was written in reference to producing counterfeit money. Explain in detail how you drew this conclusion including the relevance of CH_3COCH_3 and NaClO (what are they and how are they used?).

Department of Motor Vehicles Registration

Owner Information	
Name/Address	**Telephone**
Bolen, Patsy 808 River Road Millstadt Falls, Missouri	766-024-6868

Vehicle Information		
Make/Model	**Year**	**Color**
Honda Accord	2012	Red
Kind of Vehicle	**Body Style**	**Vehicle ID Number**
Passenger	4 door	G4KLS4X9KW33294

Registration Information		
Current Type	**Current Plate Number**	**Expiration**
Passenger Non-Van	ABC321	10/2018

Department of Motor Vehicles Registration

Owner Information	
Name/Address	**Telephone**
Graber, Robbie 123 Fishhook Lane Bass Lake, Missouri	766-100-4353

Vehicle Information		
Make/Model	**Year**	**Color**
Ford F-150XL	2012	Blue
Kind of Vehicle	**Body Style**	**Vehicle ID Number**
Truck	2 door Regular Cab	C4PWR7JLW99623

Registration Information		
Current Type	**Current Plate Number**	**Expiration**
Truck Regular Cab	LV2FSH	12/2018

Department of Motor Vehicles Registration

Owner Information	
Name/Address	**Telephone**
Hartmann, Michael 103 Tractor Lane Millstadt Falls, Missouri	766-010-0234

Vehicle Information		
Make/Model	**Year**	**Color**
Ford F-150XL	2013	Blue
Kind of Vehicle	**Body Style**	**Vehicle ID Number**
Truck	2 door Regular Cab	C4PWP7LIU99628

Registration Information		
Current Type	**Current Plate Number**	**Expiration**
Truck Regular Cab	HFS128	07/2019

Department of Motor Vehicles Registration

Owner Information	
Name/Address	**Telephone**
Young, Cheryl 214 Lynne Lane Baldwin, Illinois	111-222-3434

Vehicle Information		
Make/Model	**Year**	**Color**
Kia Optima	2015	Red
Kind of Vehicle	**Body Style**	**Vehicle ID Number**
Passenger	2 door	A2GDS3Z0GA55658

Registration Information		
Current Type	**Current Plate Number**	**Expiration**
Passenger Non-Van	CLH068	07/2019

Bass Lake Document Examiner's Office

Case Number: 033095

Preliminary Report

Case Description

On June 5, 2017, the Bass Lake Crime Scene Investigators were called to a crime scene located at the Hartmann fishing cabin at 123 Trout Lane. While investigating the scene they recovered a handwritten list in the kitchen of the cabin.

Summary of Initial Findings

The list was written on a piece of scrap paper measuring approximately 4 inches x 5 inches. The list is attached below.

Dish Pan
Gloves
Measuring Cup (ml)
Printer
Paper
CH3COCH3
NaCIO
$1 bills

Bass Lake Document Examiner's Office

Case Number: 033095 **Final Report**

You are the Senior Document Examiner on staff. Use the 12 Characteristics for Comparing Handwriting (Page 95) chart to examine each of the handwriting samples, comparing them to the questioned document to determine the author of the list found at the crime scene.

You may be called upon to testify in court and therefore will need to justify your conclusion. In the blank chart on the next page, record at least four unique characteristics found in the questioned document and the suspect sample that allowed you to determine the identity of the person writing the list.

After you have completed this chart, record your final conclusion in the space below.

Final Conclusion

1. Based on your observations, who do you believe wrote the note?

2. You will need to prepare a statement for the lead detective in this case, summarizing your findings. Using the chart you completed, describe at least 4 of the characteristics that you used to help you identify the author of the note. Give specific examples of the exact letters/words that you examined.

Analysis of the Handwriting Sample of ______________________ (Suspect's Name)

List at least 4 specific words or phrases that you examined from the handwritten list and your suspect sample, recording them in the appropriate categories below. Elaborate on those unique characteristics describing specifically what you saw (what made them unique).

Handwriting Characteristic	Specific Words or Phrases and Their Characteristics
1. Line quality	
2. Spacing of words and letters	
3. Ratio of relative height, width, and size of letters	
4. Pen lifts and separations	
5. Connecting strokes	
6. Beginning and ending strokes	
7. Unusual letter formation	
8. Shading or pen pressure	
9. Slant of letters	
10. Baseline habits	
11. Flourishes or embellishments	
12. Placement of diacritics	

Bass Lake Document Examiner's Office

Case Number: 033095

Handwriting Sample

The following handwriting sample was taken from Patsy Bolen.

Dish Pan
Gloves
Measuring Cup (ml)
Printer
Paper
CH3COCH3
NaClO
$1 bills

Bass Lake
Document Examiner's Office

Case Number: 033095 **Handwriting Sample**

The following handwriting sample was taken from Matthew Hartmann.

Dish Pan
Gloves
Measuring Cup (mL)
Printer
Paper
CH_3COCH_3
$NaClO$
$1 bills

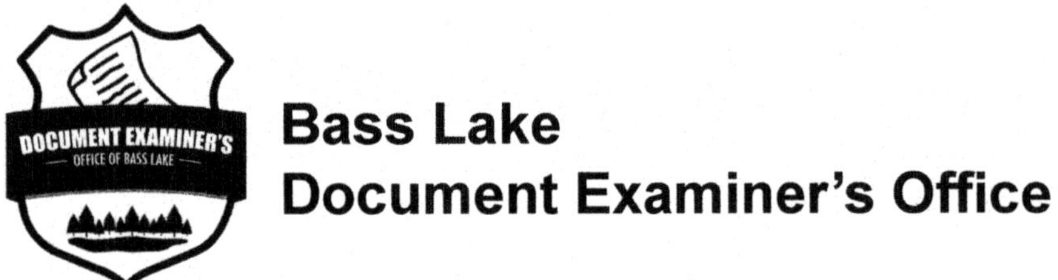

Bass Lake
Document Examiner's Office

Case Number: 033095

Handwriting Sample

The following handwriting sample was taken from Michael Hartmann.

Dish Pan
Gloves
Measuring Cup (ml)
Printer
Paper
CH_3COCH_3
NaClO
$1 bills

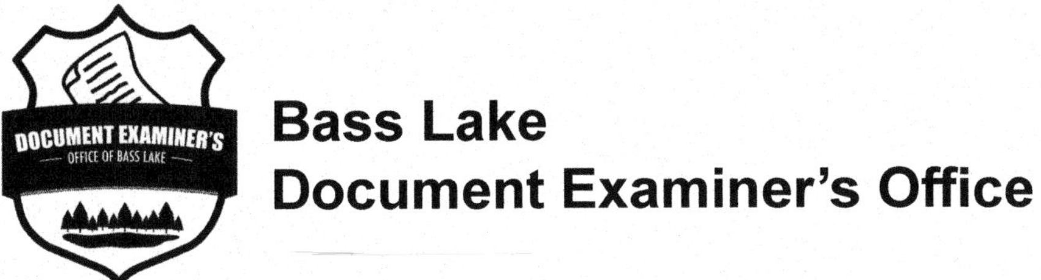

Bass Lake
Document Examiner's Office

Case Number: 033095

Handwriting Sample

The following handwriting sample was taken from Cheryl Young.

Dish Pan
Gloves
Measuring cup (ml)
Printer
Paper
CH3COCH3
NaClO
$1 bills

Bass Lake Fingerprint Examiner's Office

Case Number: 033095

Preliminary Report

Case Description

Six fingerprints were recovered from multiple areas at the Hartmann fishing cabin located at 123 Trout Lane. Those prints are documented in this report.

Print 1: Recovered from a hand gun found underneath the front porch.

Print 2: Recovered from a hand gun found in a blue Ford truck.

Print 3: Recovered from a printer found in the fishing cabin.

Print 4: Recovered from the steering wheel of the blue Ford truck.

Print 5: Recovered from the handle of the gas can found at the back of the shed.

Print 6: Recovered from the cell phone found in the kitchen in the cabin.

Bass Lake
Fingerprint Examiner's Office

Case Number: 033095 **Final Report**

You are the Senior Latent Fingerprint Examiner on staff at the fingerprint lab. Examine the fingerprints recovered from the crime scene and the prints taken from those people identified as persons of interest. Compare the samples and determine the identity of the person who left each print. Record your findings in the table provided. Summarize your findings in paragraph form.

Print Number	Location Recovered	Name of Person to Whom the Print Belongs	Digit of Identified Print (check one)		Type of Print (check one)
1	Hand gun found under the front porch		**Right Hand** ___ thumb ___ index ___ middle ___ ring ___ little	**Left Hand** ___ thumb ___ index ___ middle ___ ring ___ little	___ arch ___ loop ___ whorl
2	Hand gun found in Ford truck on property		**Right Hand** ___ thumb ___ index ___ middle ___ ring ___ little	**Left Hand** ___ thumb ___ index ___ middle ___ ring ___ little	___ arch ___ loop ___ whorl
3	Printer in fishing cabin		**Right Hand** ___ thumb ___ index ___ middle ___ ring ___ little	**Left Hand** ___ thumb ___ index ___ middle ___ ring ___ little	___ arch ___ loop ___ whorl
4	Steering wheel of Ford truck on property		**Right Hand** ___ thumb ___ index ___ middle ___ ring ___ little	**Left Hand** ___ thumb ___ index ___ middle ___ ring ___ little	___ arch ___ loop ___ whorl

Print Number	Location Recovered	Name of Person to Whom the Print Belongs	Digit of Identified Print (check one)		Type of Print (check one)
5	Handle of gas can found by shed		**Right Hand** ___ thumb ___ index ___ middle ___ ring ___ little	**Left Hand** ___ thumb ___ index ___ middle ___ ring ___ little	___ arch ___ loop ___ whorl
6	Cell phone found in cabin		**Right Hand** ___ thumb ___ index ___ middle ___ ring ___ little	**Left Hand** ___ thumb ___ index ___ middle ___ ring ___ little	___ arch ___ loop ___ whorl

Final Conclusions

1. You will need to share your findings with the lead detective in this case. Write, in sentences, the summary of your examination here. Include the location from where each print was recovered and to whom each print belongs.

2. Should you be called to testify in court:

   a. Briefly explain how fingerprints are left behind on a surface.

   b. What would you say to the jury to convince them that fingerprints are foolproof?

Bass Lake Fingerprint Examiner's Office

Name: Bolen (Last) Patsy (First) P. (Middle)

Race: Caucasian Sex: F DOB: October 9, 1991

Right Thumb	Right Index	Right Middle	Right Ring	Right Little
Left Thumb	**Left Index**	**Left Middle**	**Left Ring**	**Left Little**

SIGNATURE OF PERSON FINGERPRINTED	SIGNATURE OF OFFICIAL TAKING FINGERPRINTS
X Patsy Bolen	Christi Sanderson

Bass Lake Fingerprint Examiner's Office

Name: Graber (Last) Robbie (First) D. (Middle)

Race: Caucasian Sex: M DOB: May 30, 1986

Right Thumb	Right Index	Right Middle	Right Ring	Right Little
Left Thumb	**Left Index**	**Left Middle**	**Left Ring**	**Left Little**

SIGNATURE OF PERSON FINGERPRINTED	SIGNATURE OF OFFICIAL TAKING FINGERPRINTS
X Robbie Graber	Christi Sanderson

Bass Lake Fingerprint Examiner's Office

Name: Hartmann (Last) Matthew (First) J. (Middle)

Race: Caucasian Sex: M DOB: March 30, 1986

Right Thumb	Right Index	Right Middle	Right Ring	Right Little
Left Thumb	**Left Index**	**Left Middle**	**Left Ring**	**Left Little**

SIGNATURE OF PERSON FINGERPRINTED	SIGNATURE OF OFFICIAL TAKING FINGERPRINTS
X Matt Hartmann	Christi Sanderson

Bass Lake Fingerprint Examiner's Office

Name: Hartmann (Last) Michael (First) D. (Middle)

Race: Caucasian Sex: M DOB: December 8, 1966

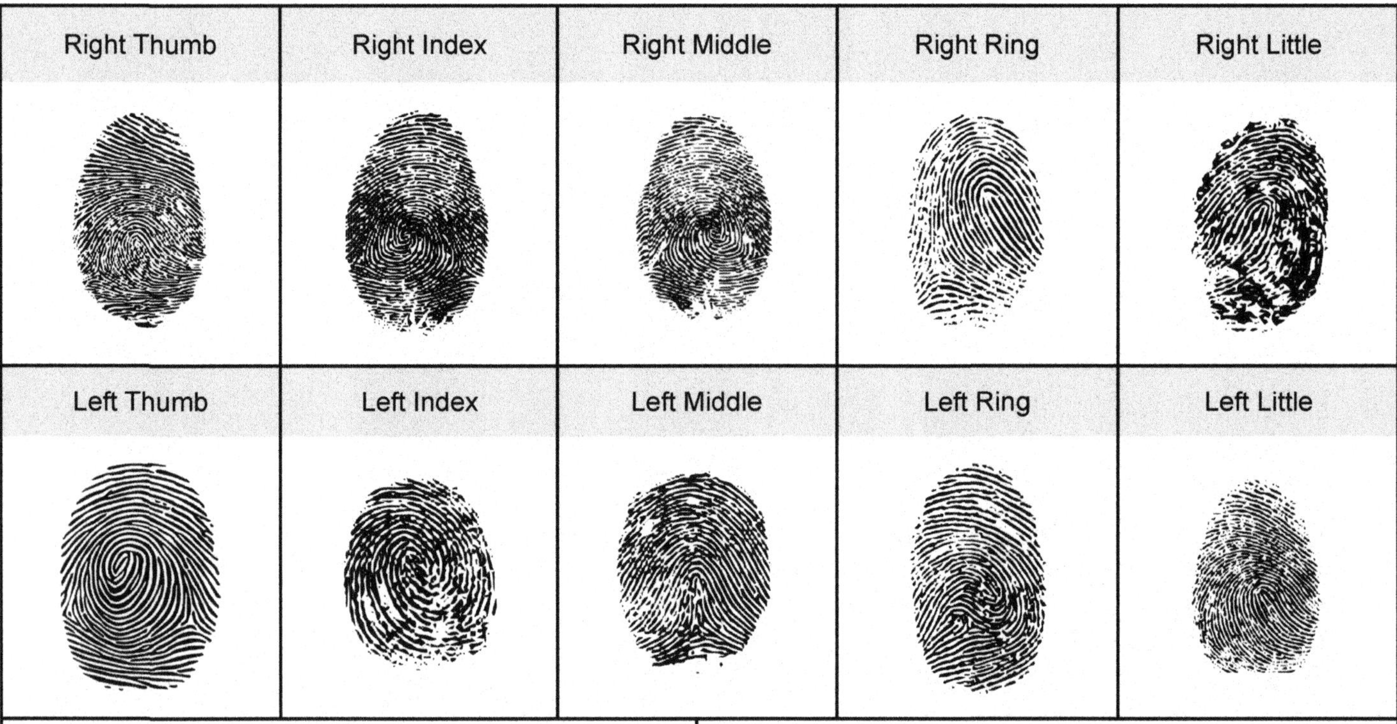

Right Thumb	Right Index	Right Middle	Right Ring	Right Little
Left Thumb	Left Index	Left Middle	Left Ring	Left Little

SIGNATURE OF PERSON FINGERPRINTED	SIGNATURE OF OFFICIAL TAKING FINGERPRINTS
X *Michael Hartmann*	*Christi Sanderson*

Bass Lake
Fingerprint Examiner's Office

Name: Hudson (Last) Andrew (First) H. (Middle)

Race: African American Sex: M DOB: November 4, 1994

Right Thumb	Right Index	Right Middle	Right Ring	Right Little
Left Thumb	**Left Index**	**Left Middle**	**Left Ring**	**Left Little**

SIGNATURE OF PERSON FINGERPRINTED	SIGNATURE OF OFFICIAL TAKING FINGERPRINTS
X Andrew Hudson	Christi Sanderson

Bass Lake
Fingerprint Examiner's Office

Name: Monty (Last) Malik (First) G. (Middle)

Race: African American Sex: M DOB: September 10, 1993

Right Thumb	Right Index	Right Middle	Right Ring	Right Little

Left Thumb	**Left Index**	**Left Middle**	**Left Ring**	**Left Little**

SIGNATURE OF PERSON FINGERPRINTED	SIGNATURE OF OFFICIAL TAKING FINGERPRINTS
X *Malik Monty*	*Christi Sanderson*

Bass Lake
Fingerprint Examiner's Office

Name: Terrington (Last) Tyler (First) F. (Middle)

Race: Caucasian Sex: M DOB: October 3, 1990

Right Thumb	Right Index	Right Middle	Right Ring	Right Little

Left Thumb	**Left Index**	**Left Middle**	**Left Ring**	**Left Little**

SIGNATURE OF PERSON FINGERPRINTED	SIGNATURE OF OFFICIAL TAKING FINGERPRINTS
X Tyler Terrington	Christi Sanderson

Bass Lake Fingerprint Examiner's Office

Name: Young (Last) Cheryl (First) L. (Middle)

Race: Caucasian Sex: F DOB: June 8, 1964

Right Thumb	Right Index	Right Middle	Right Ring	Right Little

Left Thumb	**Left Index**	**Left Middle**	**Left Ring**	**Left Little**

SIGNATURE OF PERSON FINGERPRINTED	SIGNATURE OF OFFICIAL TAKING FINGERPRINTS
X *Cheryl Young*	*Christi Sanderson*

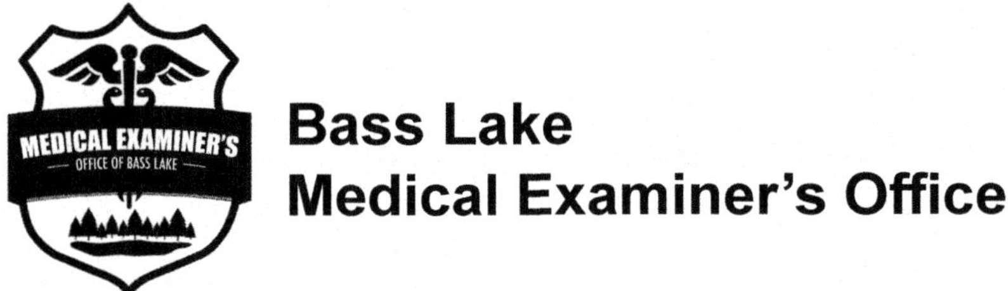

Bass Lake
Medical Examiner's Office

Case Number: 033095 **Preliminary Report**

Case Description

On June 5, 2017, the Medical Examiner's office was called to 123 Trout Lane. An unidentified dead body was found in a partially burned shed at the back of the property. The body was brought to the M.E.'s office for an autopsy. The body has yet to be identified. The following information is preliminary and subject to change as some test results are pending.

Summary of Initial Findings

1. The body was identified as being an African American male.
2. The age was estimated to be between 21 and 25 years.
3. Height was recorded as approximately 5 feet 10 inches.
4. Burns covered the lower extremities of the body.
5. Hands and fingers did not suffer any burn damage.
6. There was one bullet wound to the *back* of the head.
7. An examination of the lungs revealed they contained no smoke.
8. No drugs or poisons were found in the body.
9. Blowfly eggs were present on the body.
10. Undigested food was found in the stomach.
11. Rigor mortis was present in the body.

Cause of Death

Based on the initial examination, the victim died of a gunshot wound to the head.

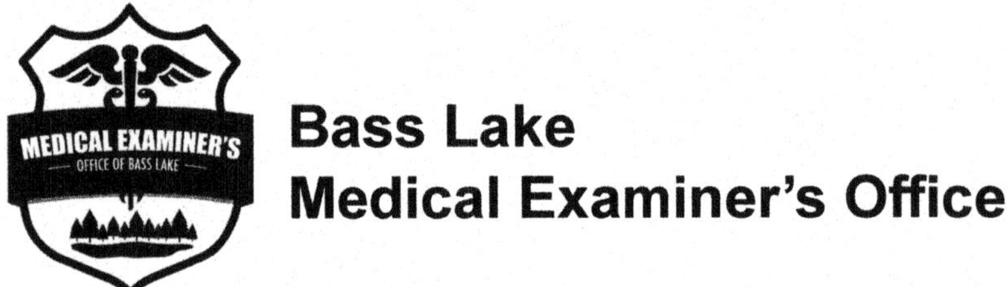

Bass Lake
Medical Examiner's Office

Case Number: 033095 **Final Report**

You are the pathologist who performed the autopsy. You must share your professional opinions with the lead detective on the case. Based on the 11 facts given in the preliminary report, what conclusions can you draw? Be specific in your explanations should you be called upon to give expert testimony in court. State your conclusions by answering the following questions.

1. You established the cause of death as a gunshot wound to the head. How did you know the victim did not die as a result of the fire?

2. When you found the body, blowfly eggs were present. Approximately how many hours had this person been deceased? Explain how you determined this.

3. Based on the stomach contents, approximately how long after eating did this person die?

4. Rigor mortis was present in the body. Approximately how many hours had this person been dead?

5. In case you are called to testify in court, please explain what rigor mortis is and what causes it.

Answer Keys

Pages 32-35

Investigation Notes Case File Number 033095

1. **Criminal Action**

   Based on what was found on the property and in the cabin, list the potential crime(s) that may have taken place.

   Answers may vary: arson, murder, counterfeit money operation

2. **Physical Evidence**

   What pieces of potential physical evidence do you see at the crime scene that you would like to further examine? List the item and give the location. Then, explain how that evidence might help you solve this case. Note: You may or may not use all of the rows in the chart.

   Answers may vary. Possible answers below.

Description of Evidence	Location Recovered	Explain How This Evidence Might Help You Solve the Case
1. Broken glass	Bedroom #1 in fishing cabin	Someone may have broken into the cabin Motive for breaking into cabin
2. Stacks of money	Closet in bedroom #1	Stolen from a bank or counterfeit money Determine what the crime is
3. High resolution printer	Bedroom #1	Used to print fake money
4. Gun	Under front porch	Might contain fingerprints, could determine who used the gun
5. iPhone	Kitchen in cabin	Belonged to whomever broke in
6. Empty gas can	Outside of shed that was on fire	Source of fire, can might contain fingerprints
7. Dead body	In shed	Might provide information about who committed the crime if we can figure out who the dead body is
8. Two bullets	Embedded in west wall of shed	Might be able to match bullet to gun, get fingerprints, and determine who fired the gun
9. Ford truck	Parked outside of burned shed	If we find the owner it might help in identifying the dead body in shed
10. Keys	In truck ignition	Might have fingerprints on keys, could help identify fire victim
11. Gun	Glove box in truck	Might contain fingerprints, could determine who used the gun
12. 4 bones	Shallow grave behind cabin	Might provide information about who committed the crime if we can figure out who the dead body is

3. **Testimonial Evidence**

What people (witnesses, neighbors, etc.) might you want to interview? List the person and describe what information you hope to gain from interviewing this person. If you don't know this person by name, then just list the relationship—neighbor, owner of cabin, etc. Note: You may or may not use all of the rows in the chart.

Answers may vary. Possible answers below.

Persons You Want to Interview	Information You Hope to Gain
1. Taylor Daniels	Eye witness might be able to identify who was at the fishing cabin near time of fire
2. Matthew Hartmann	Might have started the fire, could provide a motive for someone else to start the fire to get back at him/revenge
3. Resident of Hudson Home	Eye witness might be able to identify who was at the fishing cabin near time of fire
4. The owner of the rowboat	Eye witness might be able to identify who was at the fishing cabin near time of fire

4. **Experts/Forensic Scientists**

What experts do you need to help you with this case? What evidence will they examine? How will this help you solve this case? Note: You may or may not use all of the rows in the chart.

Answers may vary. Possible answers below.

Experts/Scientists	Evidence They May Examine and How This Might Help You Solve the Case
1. Arson expert	Determine if the fire was an accident or arson
2. Secret Service Agent	Determine if money is counterfeit
3. Fingerprint examiner	Find prints at the crime scene to identify possible suspects or identify victim
4. Medical examiner	Identify the body and determine cause of death
5. Anthropologist	Determine to whom the bones might belong
6. Ballistics	Determine type of gun and bullets used
7. Document/Handwriting examiner	Determine who wrote the list

Pages 43-44

Investigation Notes Case File Number 021394

1. **Criminal Action**

   Based on what reportedly took place at the Quik Trip, list the potential crime(s) that may have taken place.

   Answers may vary: counterfeit money was used to purchase gasoline.

2. **Physical Evidence**

   What pieces of potential physical evidence do you see at the crime scene that you would like to further examine? List the item and give the location. Then explain how that evidence might help you solve this case. Note: You may or may not use all of the rows in the chart.

   Answers may vary. Possible answers below.

Description of Evidence	Location Recovered	Explain How This Evidence Might Help You Solve the Case
1. $20 bills used to pay for gas	Given to manager at gas station	Examine to determine if a crime was committed by using counterfeit money
2. Car make/model	At gas station	Might help us figure out who owns the car and bought the gas
3. Security camera footage	Inside and outside of station	Confirm identity of car and person purchasing gas

3. **Testimonial Evidence**

   Which people might you want to interview? List the person and describe what information you hope to gain from interviewing this person. If you don't know this person by name, then just list the relationship—woman driving car, manager, etc. Note: You may or may not use all of the rows in the chart.

   Answers may vary. Possible answers below.

Persons You Want to Interview	Information You Hope to Gain
1. Karen Kaye	Describe person passing counterfeit money, as well as, make and model of car
2. Other customers at gas station	Could confirm what manager saw or give additional details

4. **Experts/Forensic Scientists**

   What experts do you need to help you with this case? What evidence will they examine? How will this help you solve this case? Note: You may or may not use all of the rows in the chart.

   Answers may vary. Possible answers below.

Expert/Scientist	Evidence to Examine that May Give Information to Help You Solve the Case
1. Secret Service	Determine if money is counterfeit
2. Fingerprint examiner	Get prints off money or gas pump handle to help identify suspect

Pages 45-46

Answers may vary. See page xv for a detailed Timeline of Events.

Pages 47-50

Case Closed: Final Report on Case Numbers 021394 and 033095

1. **Main Suspect(s)**

   List who you will be charging, describe the crime with which he/she is being charged, as well as his/her motive.

Name of Person Charged	Description of Crimes Committed	Description of Motives
Tyler Terrington	Murder of Andrew Hudson Murder of Robbie Graber	Eliminate witnesses who stumbled upon his counterfeit money making
Patsy Bolen	Passing counterfeit money Crime concealment	Part of counterfeit money crime ring Burned shed to conceal dead body

2. **Eliminated Suspects**

   During your investigation were there other people on your list of possible suspects? If so, identify them in the table below.

   Answers will vary.

3. **Victims**

   Identify each of the victims found at the crime scene and describe how you identified each person. Be detailed in your justification giving specific facts from official reports and/or witness statements.

   Answers may vary. Possible answers below.

Location of Victim	Identity of Victims (name)	Specific Facts to Support Your Conclusion
Body found in shed	Andrew Hudson	• Andrew was last seen in his rowboat and it was later found at cabin • Age and height approximations matched Andrew • Body burned in shed was African American, as was Andrew • A phone found inside the cabin contained Andrew's fingerprint • Time of death indicated at autopsy consistent with his mother's story: food found in stomach, blowfly eggs on body, body in state of rigor mortis
Bones found in shallow grave	Robbie Graber	• Length of bones match the approximate height of Robbie • Pelvic bone indicates a male • Closed sagittal suture on skull indicates a male at least 26 years of age • Shape of skull indicates Caucasian

4. **Physical Evidence**

Give the relevant facts from each department report that support the reasons why you believe the identified person(s) committed the crime.

Answers may vary. Possible answers below.

Arson: List the facts that justify the fire at the shed was arson.	**Ballistics:** Identify which guns fired which bullets, giving the location of bullets/guns.
• *Gas can found at scene* • *Color of smoke* • *Color of flame* • *Burn pattern at point of origin*	*Two bullets in west wall of shed from Sig P250* *Bullet found in dead body in shed also from Sig P250* *Bullet found by bones in shallow grave fired from the Glock 26*
Fingerprints: List whose fingerprints were found and where. • *Tyler Terrington on both guns* • *Patsy Bolen on printer and gas can* • *Robbie Graber on steering wheel of truck* • *Andrew Hudson on phone*	**Documents/Handwriting:** Tell who wrote the list and why it was important to the case. *Patsy Bolen wrote the list. It is important because it is proof that she was planning on making counterfeit money. The list included materials necessary for making fake money.*
Counterfeit Money: Describe the role this plays in the crime spree. *Two people (Graber and Hudson) were both killed because they discovered Terrington and Bolen making counterfeit money.*	**Automobile Report:** Tell who owns the car seen leaving the fishing cabin and who owns the blue truck. Describe why knowing this is important. *Patsy Bolen owns the car seen leaving the fishing cabin. This is important because it proves she was at the cabin where the counterfeit money was made and where two people were killed.*

5. **Additional Information**

As in many police investigations, some of the evidence gathered is circumstantial. And in some cases, police officers wish they had additional bits of information to help them piece together the case. Before you make your final conclusions, what additional information do you wish you had? This could be physical or testimonial evidence. Attach additional paper if needed.

Answers will vary.

6. **Summary of Final Conclusions**

Based on the information you recovered during your investigation, write a narrative describing the events that you believe took place leading up to the crimes. In other words, tell who, why, when (timeline) and how the crime(s) were committed. Write or type your narrative in complete sentences. Attach additional paper as needed.

Answers will vary.

Pages 70-71

Anthropology Department Final Report

Pelvic Bone	Belonged to a: Gender: ✓ male _____ female	Justification/How do you know? (be specific) *Narrow, long sacrum*
Skull	Belonged to a: Gender: ✓ male _____ female Race: ✓ Caucasoid _____ Negroid _____ Mongoloid Approx. age at least 26 years	Justification/How do you know? (be specific) *Chin is U-shaped, eye openings are square, brow ridge is prominent and heavy* *Cranial length is long, narrow cranial breadth, narrow nasal aperture, sloping eye orbits* *Sagittal sutures are completely closed*

Humerus Bone (38.6 cm long)	Approximately how tall (in feet and inches) is the person to whom this bone belongs? 6 ft 2 in.	Justification /How do you know?(be specific) *Formula for a male:* *38.6 x 2.99 + 72.42 = 6 feet 2 inches*
Tibia Bone (45 cm long)	Approximately how tall (in feet and inches) is the person to whom this bone belongs? 6 ft 2 in.	Justification/How do you know? (be specific) *Formula for a male:* *45 x 2.37 + 80.97 = 6 feet 2 inches*

Final Conclusion: You will need to prepare a statement for the lead detective in this case. Describe the person to whom you believe the bones belong giving the gender, race, age, and approximate height. Write your profile in a sentence. (For example, "The bones belong to a ....")

Based on the characteristics identified in the report, the bones belong to a Caucasoid male, height approximately 6 feet 2 inches tall, and at least 26 years of age.

Pages 73-74

Arson Department Final Report

1. Where was the origin of the fire? Explain how you arrived at your conclusion.

   The origin of the fire was at the back of the shed based upon the V-burn formation found there.

2. What conclusion can you draw based on the color of the smoke? Be specific.

   The color of the smoke was thick and black which would indicate that an accelerant such as gasoline was used to start the fire.

3. What conclusion can you draw from observing the color of the flame? Be specific.

   The flames were yellowish-white which means the fire was burning between approximately 1,825 to 2,200 degrees. Since a normal house fire burns at approximately 1,550 degrees, this would indicate an accelerant was used to get the fire to burn hotter.

4. What conclusion can you draw from finding the presence of crazing on the windows in the shed? Be specific.

   Small crazing would indicate a hot, fast fire which means an accelerant was used.

5. Copper wires were melted during the fire. What does this indicate? Be specific.

   Copper melts at 1,981 degrees which means it was burning hotter than a normal house fire, so an accelerant was used.

6. How does knowing the temperature at which the fire was burning help you determine whether or not the fire was accidental or an act of arson? Be specific.

   If the temperature is over 1,550 degrees then the fire had an accelerant to make it burn faster. This would indicate the fire was an act of arson.

Final Conclusion: You will need to prepare a statement for the lead detective in this case. In your professional opinion, was this an act of arson or an accidental fire? Justify your answer using information reported on the preliminary report. Be very detailed in your justification, giving at least 4 reasons to support your claim. Write your statement in paragraph form.

Answers may vary. Possible answer: This fire was an act of arson. Investigators saw a V burn pattern at the back of the shed which would indicate the origin of the fire. The smoke was thick and black which means an accelerant was used. The flame color was yellowish-white and copper wires were melted which shows the fire was burning hotter than a normal house fire. In addition, the windows contained crazing, another indicator of a fast hot fire.

Pages 76-77

Ballistics Department Final Report

Firearms

Write the name of the make of the guns recovered from the scene.

Gun 1: Recovered from under the front porch Make: GLOCK 26

Gun 2: Recovered from the Ford truck Make: SIG P250

Bullets

Write the caliber of the bullets recovered from each location.

Bullet 1: West wall of shed Caliber: 9mm

Bullet 2: West wall of shed Caliber: 9mm

Bullet 3: Dead body in shed Caliber: 9mm

Bullet 4: In shallow grave Caliber: 9mm

Number and Location of Bullet	Gun That Fired This Bullet (identify by make)
Bullet 1 (embedded in west wall of shed)	Sig P250
Bullet 2 (embedded in west wall of shed)	Sig P250
Bullet 3 (dead body in shed)	Sig P250
Bullet 4 (shallow grave)	GLOCK 26

Final Conclusion: You will need to prepare a statement for the lead detective in this case, summarizing your findings after inspecting all guns and bullets associated with this case. Write your summary in paragraph form, describing which gun fired which bullet. Include the location from which the bullet was recovered.

The 9mm bullets found in the west wall of the shed and in the body in the shed were all fired from the same gun, the Sig P250. This gun was found in the Ford truck on the property. The GLOCK 26, fired a 9mm bullet that was recovered in the shallow grave. This gun was found under the front porch of the cabin.

Page 85

Counterfeit Currency Division's Preliminary Report 021394

Conclusion: *counterfeit*

Page 86

Counterfeit Currency Division's Final Report 021394

1. The counterfeit detection pen left a black mark on the bills that were examined. Explain why that happens in counterfeit money.

   The ink in the pen contains an iodine solution that reacts with the starch in wood-based paper.

2. Your investigation revealed there was no watermark on the bill. In a real $20 what should the watermark look like?

   Andrew Jackson

3. The 20 at the lower left of the bill remained a solid color when the bill was shifted. What should have happened when the bill was shifted?

   The ink should have shifted from copper to green in color.

4. There was no evidence of a security thread when the $20 bill was exposed to UV light. What color of security thread should have been on the bill?

   The security thread is green.

5. When examined, no clear micro-printing was found. Give two examples of where you would expect to see micro-printing on a $20 bill, as well as what it should say.

   Answers may vary:

   - *"THE UNITED STATES OF AMERICA 20 USA" in the border below Treasurer's signature*
   - *"USA20" borders beginning part of text ribbon*
   - *"USA TWENTY" to right of portrait*

Page 87

Counterfeit Currency Division's Preliminary Report 033095

Conclusion: *counterfeit*

Page 88

Counterfeit Currency Division's Final Report 033095

1. The counterfeit detection pen left a yellowish mark on the bill but yet you determined the bill to be counterfeit. Explain how this is possible.

   The counterfeiter could have bleached a real bill and then printed the counterfeit bill over it.

2. The bill contained embedded red and blue fibers consistent with real money but yet you determined the bill to be counterfeit. Explain how this is possible.

   The counterfeiter could have bleached a real bill and then printed the counterfeit bill over it.

3. Your investigation revealed there was no watermark on the bill. If the counterfeiters did indeed bleach a bill and then print on top of it what denomination did they use? Explain how you know.

   The counterfeiters must have used a $1 bill because that is the only denomination that doesn't have a watermark as a security feature.

4. A handwritten list was also recovered from the crime scene. After reading the contents of this list you determined that it was written in reference to producing counterfeit money. Explain in detail how you drew this conclusion including the relevance of CH3COCH3 and NaClO (what are they and how are they used?).

   CH3COCH3 and NaClO are both chemicals that are used to dissolve or bleach the ink printed on paper money. The counterfeiters needed these chemicals to remove the existing ink from $1 bills. They then printed $20 bills using the paper from the $1 bills.

Page 94

Document Examiner's Final Report

Final Conclusion

1. Based on your observations, who do you believe wrote the note?

   Patsy Bolen

2. You will need to prepare a statement for the lead detective in this case, summarizing your findings. Using the chart you completed, describe at least 4 of the characteristics that you used to help you identify the author of the note. Give specific examples of the exact letters/words that you examined.

   Answers will vary.

Page 95

Answers may vary.

Page 101-102

Fingerprint Examination Final Report

Print Number	Location Recovered	Name of Person to Whom the Print Belongs	Digit of Identified Print (check one)	Type of Print (check one)
1	Hand gun found under the front porch	Tyler Terrington	Right thumb	loop
2	Hand gun found in Ford truck on property	Tyler Terrington	Right ring	whorl
3	Printer in fishing cabin	Patsy Bolen	Left ring	whorl
4	Steering wheel of Ford truck on property	Robbie Graber	Right index	whorl
5	Handle of gas can found by shed	Patsy Bolen	Left thumb	arch
6	Cell phone found in cabin	Andrew Hudson	Right middle	loop

Final Conclusions

1. You will need to share your findings with the lead detective in this case. Write, in sentences, the summary of your examination here. Include the location from where each print was recovered and to whom each print belongs.

   The fingerprints of Tyler Terrington were found on both guns that were recovered at the crime scene. One gun was found under the front porch, while the other gun was found in truck on the property. Patsy Bolen's fingerprints were found on a laser printer in the Hartmann fishing cabin, as well as on a gas can located near the shed on the property. After dusting the interior of the truck for prints, one was found on the steering wheel. This print belonged to Robbie Graber. Finally, a cell phone found on the kitchen table in the fishing cabin contained a fingerprint of Andrew Hudson.

2. Should you be called to testify in court:

   a. Briefly explain how fingerprints are left behind on a surface.

      Fingerprints are left behind on surfaces because of the sweat glands and ridges on our fingers. When we touch something a small amount of the oils are left on the surface of the object we touched in the pattern of our ridges.

   b. What would you say to the jury to convince them that fingerprints are foolproof?

      Fingerprints are considered foolproof because every person has unique fingerprints.

Page 112

Medical Examiner's Office Final Report

1. You established the cause of death as a gunshot wound to the head. How did you know the victim did not die as a result of the fire?

   The lungs were free of smoke, which means the victim was already dead when placed in the fire.

2. When you found the body, blowfly eggs were present. Approximately how many hours had this person been deceased? Explain how you determined this.

   The body had been deceased approximately 24 hours or less. I know this because of the life cycle of a blow fly. Flies lay eggs within the first day that a body dies.

3. Based on the stomach contents, approximately how long after eating did this person die?

   Undigested food was found in the stomach which suggests the person died within 2 hours after eating his/her last meal.

4. Rigor mortis was present in the body. Approximately how many hours had this person been dead?

   This person had been dead for at least 2 hours and at most 48 hours.

5. In case you are called to testify in court, please explain what rigor mortis is and what causes it.

   Rigor mortis is when the body becomes stiff after death. This happens because the skeletal muscles become locked or stiff and are unable to relax for a period of time after death.